Beyond Belief
The Trick of the Time-mind

Deon .V. J. Ashton

A word or two regarding copyright

The law of copyright asserts that 'Intellectual Property' is a quantifiable and identifiable aspect of life that exists as the exclusive ownership of an individual. This is a concept that is rooted in an objective world view which sees all constituent 'parts' remote from one another. As all that truly exists is one whole undivided unicity in which there can be no infringement or encroachment of one aspect upon another. Nor can there be any claim of individual intellectual sovereignty . 'Safeguards' such as copyright simply serve to reinforce this illusory idea of isolation and it's counterpart, vulnerability.

This volume asserts to the contrary and is therefore, free of all copyright restriction.

ISBN 978-1-4116-0849-8

To Mom

Thelma Ann Ashton

Without whom these words would not
have been written.

Contents

1	Introduction	1
2	The nature of self	3
3	My world of belief	13
4	Someone in time	19
5	Ambiguity	27
6	My temporal self	33
7	Pretend Personality	39
8	Delusion of division	45
9	Aspirations and Evaluations	49
10	The Particular Perspective	53
11	Death of future promise	61
12	The Spiritual Journey	71
13	Resistance	75
14	Acceptance	79
15	The Roller Coaster	83
16	Why am I here?	87
17	Reflections	95
18	Playground polarities	99
19	The Tree	103
20	The Pool	109
21	Goal Orientation	113
22	The life of avoidance	119
23	Content and confusion	123
24	The Imagination of Psychology	127
25	My precious opinion	135
26	Now	143
27	Love	147
	Dialogues	153

*This world is the offspring of the
Eternal's thought; thus the
Eternal is the Real in all things.
Behold it thus with mind full
of peace. Being, free of form,
seen everywhere. Knowers of
the Eternal understand that
whatever is other than this,
is but the sport and workmanship
of intellect.*

Śankarâchârya

Introduction

*It is certain that the nature of the mind is
empty and without any foundation whatsoever.
Your own mind is insubstantial like the empty sky.*

Padmsambhava

The following reflections examine the nature of human existence and it's source, looking at the condition of the apparent individual and it's creation within time. Without prescriptive direction or intent, the stance taken is one of open enquiry. There is no claim of 'ultimate Truth' being divulged, for the absolute could never be approached in this, or any like manner. Attempting to describe the infinite with symbolism and intellectual concept is simply impossible - for they are truly incompatible - yet here is yet another volume undertaking to do just that. This is the contradiction that is at the heart of all enquiries of this nature, simply because this perplexing paradox cannot be reconciled from the standpoint of the individual, and yet it is this very sense of individuality or isolation that gives birth to the seeker and his consequent search for meaning in life. For all specifics and particulars are merely appearances of being, which is, by its very nature, whole and complete.

All that can be done, is to turn the enquiry back upon the nature of the one who seems to enquire and this is where this small volume stands. Attempting to uncover the reality behind this 'me,' this elusive self that would claim volitional ownership of the thoughts it thinks and actions it takes, within a seemingly finite, linear lifespan.

What is contained within these pages therefore, is yet more '*sport and workmanship of the intellect,*' constructs of thought and symbol; concepts joined as a narrative which form part of this immediate experience of existence. Whether it is of value or merit is pure supposition, for it simply forms further fabric and fascination for the story of life. Perhaps it is best described as a pointer to the immediacy and intimacy of being itself, beyond ideas of identity, conditioning and belief, to the unconditioned nature at the heart of existence.

The Nature of Self

This world is nothing but a dance of shadows,
A line drawn between darkness and light,
Joy and oppression,
Time and eternity.
Learn to read this subtle line
For it tells all the secrets of creation.

Fakhruddin Araqi

What is life? The eternal enquiry of the thinking mind. What is life, and moreover, who is this one that lives it? What answer can satisfy this unquenchable thirst to simply know one's own source and reason for being? What intellect could grasp and translate the enormity of the unfathomable, of the infinite nature of being itself? Indeed, how can the unknowable be known? This is the paradox we set out with upon our quest to seek answers to those seemingly perplexing questions. Yet what may be uncovered within this enquiry is something amazingly immediate and blindingly obvious. What may be discovered is that that which was regarded as incredibly illusive, is in fact compellingly intimate and immediate.

For there is a quality of restlessness within the individual, a tangible sense of unease which seems to be a catalyst for this search for the meaning to life. It is this inherent unease which is fundamental in the very formation of the seekers nature; an agitation that gives rise to this deeper enquiry into the very nature and cause of life itself, which can be translated as the ageless search for 'God' or The Creator of this 'self.'

Yet even within this restlessness of activity a self-evident transitory nature to life can be glimpsed. Steeped in it's continual swing from striving to fulfilling, success to disappointment, ambition to attainment. It is this perpetual chasing of pleasure which characterises temporal life, a seeking that can become ultimately dissatisfying, creating that motivation (perhaps) to look at what lies at the root of this existence and to seek for a more meaningful reality beyond appearances.

'Reality' however, is an illusive creature indeed. For it seems to hide within the very fabric of life, transparent, yet present everywhere, it rests in each and every fibre and function of being, yet it cannot be touched, tasted nor possessed, still the hunger and thirst for it's peaceful embrace beckons.

The Nature of Self

In our efforts to understand this longing which is actually beyond intellectual comprehension, great symbolic narratives have been born, religions and philosophies championed by the learned and devout. Yet despite all these confounding and ultimately misleading preponderances, our longings, our deep desire to know our true ground of being seems as elusive as ever.

What we are dealing with here is the ultimate paradox of course. For existence itself is only an idea, a concept or product of mind, an intellectual movement if you will. For ultimately that which is seeking answers is nothing other than an idea within an idea. And herein lies the perplexity and ambiguity of this enquiry, this is where the chasing of the proverbial tail begins. For this apparent world of form and function, this appearance of objective reality, is nothing other than a world of interpretation in which observable 'facts' masquerade in a deception of space- time limitation.

Despite all our grand religio-symbolic stories and intellectual contrivances which seek to make sense of this paradox, there is something that becomes immediately apparent upon simple observation of one's own being; a very ordinary yet astonishingly obvious quality that requires no historical or intellectual reference, something that can be all too easily overlooked, that of *spontaneous occurrence*. With simple observation of the thought process, there is the immediate revealing of something quite extraordinary yet perplexingly ordinary - *my very own identity is nothing other than a construct of this chain of mental activity*. That which we term 'mind' is simply the continual arising of spontaneous thought, giving birth (in time) to a fictitious character I term 'me.' Each aspect of 'my identity' is locked into this sense of continuity, a linear story of beginnings and endings, of happenings in the past and hopes for the future, all connected by a narrative to form the history of 'my' life story. Yet all of these mental constructs only ever occur *right at this very moment.*

In stepping beyond this temporal and fictitious character-play of mind that has become the normal way of engaging with life, in recognising the retrospective and anticipatory nature of these thoughts, in seeing the wholly temporal and imaginary nature of this story teller, the walls of misunderstanding begin to crumble. The potency of this 'narrator mind' begins to wane, and what remains is the astonishingly ordinary and present awareness of being, right now.

Even more amazing and blindingly obvious is the fact that this awareness, this reality of being, has never been absent for a single moment. It is simply the narrative of the mind forming the idea of an independent or separate character; an intellectual assumption given a false credibility and authority. A subject-object orientation placing 'me' in isolation to an exterior and autonomous world 'out there,' a fictitious separation with a wholly false perspective, creating this isolated entity being the source and fuel of its own unease, striving and restlessness.

So is this what is meant by the term enlightenment - a simple seeing through the complex paraphernalia of the mind? Well, temporally speaking 'enlightenment' has been seen as many things; a remarkably

Hi Craig,

Here's a copy of one of my misprinted consignment (see back cover) but content is as okay as I could do. I know there are one or two errors. I won't say I hope you 'enjoy' it, cos its not like a personality could — (you'll kind of see what I mean.)

Anyway just to wish you peace in the now 😊

All the very best.

D.

illusive state attained only by the elite or fortunately selected few super-humans throughout the ages. It has been held as the pinnacle achievement of the striving and effort made by many a religious devotee. Yet this to is simply another recreation of the mind within the story of life. For enlightenment is indeed the recognition of the immediacy of being, free of all mental concoction. There is nothing extraordinary in the rediscovery of this immediate and true nature of existence, yet the hurdle of complexity is the smoke screen the mind creates in order to make the obvious nature of things seem remote and mysterious. For the term 'enlightenment' has become imbued with a rich and mysterious characteristic, suggesting few should even embark upon it's realisation.

You may even find that your mind has a resistance to this concept of 'simple enlightenment.' For there can be a great opposition to the idea of there *not* being some explosive super-human life changing event to this 'Self-realisation.' For if it were a simple case of seeing clearly and presently the way things really are, then the egoic mind's days as neurotic ruler of the kingdom would be well and truly numbered. But let's remember that there is nothing wrong with neurosis or any other form of thinking or behaviour for that matter. This is not a debate about change of appearance, but rather the examination of the very nature of this thinking entity itself and the role it plays within this seeming temporal experience.

As we will find, this enquiry can never be directed to a specific locale as such, but only focussed on this very moment and all it contains - at the one who seems to experience, rather than the experience itself. And if it is discovered that the mind really is only a flow of thoughts in time, a collection of instantaneous impulses, then what are the implications to 'my' life, and just where do 'I' fit in within this world of intellectual make-believe?

Well, lets see. If present being is all there is, then no longer can the promise of future pleasure be held ransom to present suffering, as the two are exposed as both sides of the same coin. Simple present observation is all that stands between suffering and peace; between darkness and so called 'enlightenment.' When a life event is seen with clarity as simply the event occurring absent of any superimposed dialogue, an event with its own inherent texture and flavour, then it can be fully lived and enjoyed thus. The mind however will spin it's own colourful stories to accompany these events, placing limitation and particular perspective upon the action, giving the experience a sense of continuity, association or connection with other circumstances or thoughts. And so the personality is formed in time and is experienced from this linear outlook.

It is possible then, that through simple observation of the thought process and its continual dialogue, that this central theme of *spontaneous action* or *natural occurrence* can be revealed, from which a natural self-realisation may or may not arise – for the 'self' that would be 'realised' is a phantom in the first place and hence any awakening can in no way be claimed by 'anyone' as such. Rather than there being any ambitious requirement for self-improvement or enhancement of any kind, the doer or chooser of the action is seen through, the illusion dissolved in clarity. This recognition of the fundamental nature of life as it is already happening, as distinct from the idea of improvement or circumstantial change is totally at odds with the individual mind, because it is left redundant within the sheer simplicity or ordinariness of present being. No longer having a role to play, a goal to reach, or a war to wage, it simply has no foothold and must ultimately recede into the fathomless silence of being.

For example, if there is an examination of they way things are right now, in this very instant, all that can be said is that these words are appearing in being-ness – in awareness, *right here, right now*; the only place and time that ever truly exists. And whilst it may seem that a story is linked to how 'you' came to be engaging with this text, along with historical detail as to your physical locale and so forth, it remains quite accurate to state that the only reality, as such, is this present manifestation of intellectual engagement within this present moment - The here and now. All else is manufactured mental association - a fiction or overlay to what is; a story that seems to offer the appearance of continuity and coherence within an orderly movement of time.

This mental skulduggery however, is simply an intellectual concoction, a fantasy. The appearance in time of the continuum of thought is actually a totally spontaneously arising occurrence.

In seeing this obvious and immediate nature of being; a freedom or sense of liberation may arise (equally it may not), a freedom borne out of the sense that all is occurring effortlessly - completely naturally -

life arising in the only way it can. Now the battle to right wrongs, to struggle against the tide of bad fortune can be seen for the narrative it is (though the action does not necessarily have to change at all). The intrinsic freedom from characterisation within this simplicity of seeing is what we are speaking of; A clarity and liberation in observing without attachment to outcome. Without the feeling or need to alter or grasp for experience, for life can be seen, at last, for the immediate pleasure of being itself, and accepted in all its forms and appearances.

In exposing the mind for what it is, the story-teller linking past and future, creating a character or entity within the drama to whom things happen - taking only this immediate perspective - strips away the gravity or potency of the action, revealing life happening quite ordinarily in present awareness. Nothing has changed materially or essentially, other than the narrative has been seen in its true light – simple story telling.

This exposes the altogether false assumption of projected happiness. Happiness which remains forever anticipated, lost in the grip of time's promise. For everything is present in the immediacy of this moment. It is the remarkably ordinary recognition that *all there is* lies in the one place the mind can never seek it – the reality of *this moment.*

So this text then, is a reminder that the 'you' that you believe yourself to be, is a mere hallucination, borne of memory and fuelled by desire. An invitation perhaps, to suspend belief in all that you thought you were, revealing a self that is wholly a construct of mental

The Nature of Self

association, an impostor-self; a dreamweaver; a master illusionist claiming all action and decisions of life for its own and yet remaining a truly impotent charlatan, possessing no choice whatsoever. A puppet of existence – a fabricated character within the temporal play of life.

My World of Belief

There is no effect in the exterior world that does not spring from an inner source. There is no motion that does not first occur within the mind

(Seth) Jane Roberts

In any debate upon the nature of existence it is wise to look at the fundamental assumptions that are taken as present reality and see if it is upon a solid foundation that they stand.

In the story of 21st century life on earth for example, it seems we are discovering through both scientific investigation in the field of quantum physics, and through more esoteric inward retrospection, (though they are ultimately one and the same) that science and spirituality are becoming inseparable. We are finding that we live in a world of mind, of concept, of idea. No longer is it the age of the atom, for now we have delved deeper into the mysteries of life and discovered even smaller building blocks of existence within the microcosm, so small in fact, that these particles with unfamiliar, strange sounding names like 'quarks and leptons' are simply not measurable by current methods. As Deepak Chopra once commented these particles are not even particles at all but.. *'they are more akin to electrical impulses, thoughts or Ideas.'* It is therefore, quite reasonable, (even given this most rudimentary and somewhat limited scientific evaluation) to say that we dwell in an world constructed entirely of thought. A world where physical matter is nothing other than *product of mind.*

The symbolic biblical opener *'In the beginning was the 'word''* gives a hint to this reality, pointing to the initial primordial thought; that very first self-contemplative spark from which all other thought arose, having been created in the 'image and likeness' of it's originating cause.

So at outset we are confronted with quite a conundrum. This objective world I seem to see 'out there' is really made up of thought, of impulse and not of inert and autonomous substance. Clearly if I turn this same examination upon myself, and likewise seek to find the source and origination of 'me,' I am confounded by a similar mystery within my very own being, for I simply cannot discover a physical locale in which I dwell.

I recently asked some friends to state where they felt they existed, as exactly as they were able to. After much deliberation they came to the consensus that the only true statement that they could give, that was beyond equivocation, was simply 'here' – they each existed 'here.' And at the same time it is true also that my experience as the questioner was likewise 'here' also! Within this seemingly inexplicable holographic experience there simply *is* no other statement that can elaborate upon one's immediate self-awareness without stepping into the murky waters of the objective world view. And so it is. There is absolutely no specific centre as such, to where I begin and end outside of 'here,' though it *appears* I am housed within this physical vessel. But when I really delve into this enquiry and seek to define just where 'I' exist, I seem to have this peculiarly nebulous quality. It seems, remarkably, that I must conclude that 'I' too exist as idea and concept, for I can offer no real or categorical evidence for the specific location for this 'me-ness' beyond the obvious statement 'here.'

Even the mind that thinks these thoughts, that transcribes these words, seems to be that self same flow of impulse and action. The only definitions I have for myself are pure theory, pure speculation and belief, based upon appearance given meaning by historical reference. Time being the datum by which order is apparently structured in my world.

I can, of course, agree to biological scientific definitions and descriptions of the body and it's specific function, but this again is based only upon objective mental understanding, on interpretation and intellectual processes. Ultimately, if this objective view is abandoned, I am always left with the strange ambiguity of my own existence.

So, it would be fair to say at this juncture that both I and the world I seem to encounter, are made of the same stuff – thought. Following on from this, we could argue further that all natural, universal laws of existence are nothing other than agreed concepts or beliefs. If there is no objective independent world out there, then we are living entirely at the centre of a realm of pure make-believe. We are living within a fiction, a storytelling world in which both stage and character are products of one universal mind. Rather like an ocean forming waves and ripples of form and movement, but essentially existing within one vast and indivisible mass, neither separated by distance nor time, all existing at one time in one place - Here and now, the infinite and eternal .

Of course the obvious conclusion that may be drawn from all of this is that our very creaturehood is itself an idea – a notion, that the fictitious nature of personal human life and it's inherent drama, is not quite as serious and stable as first thought and that the boundaries of fact and limitation are as vague or as definite as the mind that gives rise to them.

If the nature of a particular mind was coloured, for example, with a rigid mental belief, such as a staunch religious ideology steeped in concepts of judgement and retribution, containing an invincible wrathful God at the centre of proceeding, having power over all creation. Then this whole debate may be viewed as an affront to this all-mighty Deity. And yet it is the conditioned mind containing these beliefs which proceeds to project this stance into the apparent objective world it seems to encounter. Perhaps it is simply summed up in the often used phrase "the world you see is the world you be.'

My World of Belief

So just what is this thinking entity, and if all life consists and arises from it, through self-contemplation you could say, then clearly an investigation into the nature of this mind would seem a worthy departure.

Someone in Time

Without going out of the door one can know the whole world, Without glancing through the window one can see the ways of Heaven, The further one goes, the less one knows.

(Tao Te Ching)

If I am, and this world is, a product of mind, then who's mind and how and why did it all start? Of course if there exists just one mind, one wholly undivided beingness, then clearly there is no time and no place that ever existed where you weren't (despite what mental projections might suggest). For the here and now would be all there is and hence no *where* other than *here* to get to or from, and of course no time in which to do so. And so questions of beginnings and endings are moot, only relevant to a mind rooted in the idea of its own isolation, separated and fragmented, within a subject-object orientation, apart from its environment and other apparent entities or physical manifestations. Could this single delusional idea of isolation be where all questions of an existential nature begin? Perhaps a more pertinent enquiry would be to ask: Why would existence itself require a beginning and ending at all? Indeed, why the continual search for something outside of this present moment?

This search or seeking is the intellectual game of fascination. The mind *is* intellect at play. The story telling mind peddles in this fascination of pure fiction, it is it's life and delight, the perpetual seeking and not finding within this circular recreation of creaturehood. However, there is a fundamental difference between *knowing* it is a story and not knowing, which makes a world of difference to the engagement with it. For example, if the mind adopted the idea of being an isolated character with the belief in it's own ultimate annihilation, rather than seeing it only as an *appearance* within infinite existence, which was neither real nor in an way a threat to it's integrity or true identity. Then undoubtedly this would change the entire experience from one of carefree enjoyment to one of trepidation, anxiety and vulnerability perhaps. (The latter is the usual world view of course, and one which gives rise to implementation of safety measures and protective posturing from the threatening external environment.)

Exclusive personal investment in one's own identity (the egoic state) absent of a broader understanding of the true nature of self, is what is being spoken of. Rather like seeing through a coloured or distorted lens which imposes a particular perspective, it flavours the dish of life in a particular way. Presence is without colour or flavour or texture, beyond form and function, though embracing and encompassing all, being the source and substance of all that is. 'My' sense of personality is borne purely of a mind steeped in conditioned fragmentation and division, a state of mind that would deny the beauty and sanctity of it's own eternal wholeness.

To recognise the limited is to avail of the Limitless.

We have a seemingly unquestioned belief in this sense of 'me,' despite having no real idea of where or what it is exactly! But so attached can we be to this mental character, to this idea of self, that to question it's validity, to confront the concept of one's very own identity is often viewed as a total absurdity, or at the very least an affront to sensible rationality. The player, as an object within the play, is taken as the fundamental reality and not seen in it's true light – as simply an appearance of being.

Of course the view of the conditioned mind and it's opinions, it's sense of morality, justice, rights and wrongs and all it's conditioned beliefs, all seem so powerful and so very important in making the character what it is. And yet these characteristics are all inextricably linked to one simple concept – the idea of who I think I am within the subject-object environment. Without this conditioned state, without this particular perspective, all these relative values are merely appearances within the functioning of total unison. In the conditioned state of the personality, the unconditioned true nature of Self is obscured (though ever-present), thoughts of isolation and particular perspective are simply features of the drama.

The individual identity is a product of the storytelling mind, a polarised relative view, and though an undeniably captivating drama, it remains a wholly misleading vision when experienced in isolation.

The conditionings and beliefs that arise from mental associations that are made throughout 'my' life, become a richly textured and a totally believable narrative, both pleasurable, and at times painful – plainly it is the story which makes me, me!

So to entertain the possibility of the whole scenario being a fantasy, whilst initially difficult to accept, is perhaps the first step towards the recognition of the true nature of Self. But it is a step that will occur or otherwise, spontaneously, as the story of life unfolds. 'My' involvement in the process is as much a fabrication as the idea of 'process' itself.

So, let us examine this self. Just who is this 'me' this label of identity, this doer of the action. Where do 'I' really reside in all of this life-play that often seems like a relentless cycle of struggle. Who, or more accurately, *what* am I within all of this drama?

To get to the root of this enquiry we can use a very simple exercise that reveals immediately an amazingly obvious fact; that *the personality only exists after the event*. In other words *who* you think you are, your identity, is totally dependent upon a retrospective mental posture, or more simply a mind appearing in time, or the 'Time-mind' as it will be referred to here. For the mind, the intellect, is a product of time, without which it has no existence. It is this Time-mind that commentates on seemingly temporal events only *after* they have occurred, or in anticipation *before* they arise.

To illustrate this point perhaps you would like to try this very short exercise:

Find a quiet place and sit in silence, be quite still for a few moments with your eyes open or closed as you prefer, and simply see if you can direct the flow of thoughts that arise. See if you can find this orchestrator of thought, this 'self.' There's no need to attach a label like 'meditation' to this searching, but simply sit and see if you can pin down where 'you' are and where your involvement in the process of thought direction lies.

There is no effort required in this exercise, only an honest enquiry. Simply sit for as short or as long a period as you wish... and observe.

…..Okay, so what did you come up with, if anything? Maybe no answers came immediately to mind. Perhaps you just became caught up with physical sensations such as breathing, maybe the mind registered your heart beating, perhaps it registered aches and pains, itches, coolness and heat upon the skin. Or maybe it became totally occupied and identified with thoughts arising; mental pictures wandering from bizarre abstraction to mundane everyday concerns that just swept it away from this enquiry altogether. But just where were you within the process of the thoughts that arose? Can you categorically state you found yourself in any real sense as director of those thoughts or did you seem to evaporate into the story, becoming entangled within the dialogue?

So if you were unable to direct the flow of thoughts, where were you? Perhaps, as suggested earlier and in terms of locale, you are lead to feel that 'you' exist within the body, the physical apparatus. That would seem to be a reasonable and quite natural assumption to make. Quite clearly all physical sensations and experiences that arise even whilst sitting in relative calm and silence, seem to be experienced by 'you'. But despite 'your' best efforts it was surely impossible to locate this entity of self outside of the simplicity of the term 'here.' Indeed you may have found that the exercise demonstrated just how independently and automatically these thoughts appeared. A stream meandering this way and that, thoughts that were either observed and found to dissipate, or clung too and followed, merging this sense of self into still more mental tributaries of abstraction, before 'you came back' to observe the intellectual scenery once again.

All we can say is that the movement of thought arises, but who could ever really claim them as their own? Did 'I' instigate each impulse? Absolutely not. 'I' simply have no control over the thoughts that arise. They arrive and are followed or they arrive and are not followed. Either way 'I' do not invite them or otherwise. Whilst it *appears* that there is some kind of connection at times, some fluidity of thought, still they arise quite spontaneously.

I would strongly suggest that this little exercise shows us very quickly a fundamental truth – *we cannot locate ourselves outside of time. We seem to appear after the thought arises and only then claim it as our own. We simply do not choose thoughts* – They are not 'our thoughts' at the instant they arise. I would suggest further that if you are truly honest you will agree with these findings; that the thoughts that arose did so totally spontaneously, without invitation, and whilst one thought may *seem* to lead to another in that kind of mental continuity, ultimately all that can be said with any real accuracy is that thoughts simply arise without any direction or volition – or perhaps that the *mind seems to have a mind of its own*! And herein lies the root of our enquiry. Not only am 'I' not able to pin point where 'I' am in all of this activity, but I also notice this phenomena called 'mind' is nothing other than a steam of unprompted impulses. Even this term 'mind' is a concept in the same way as 'I' appear to be!

At this early stage we can already see that we are dealing with some very tricky and somewhat vague concepts that have been taken for granted as existent reality. Yet we are peddling in ideas, notions, phantoms even. Both 'mind' and 'me' simply cannot be located, anywhere, how very strange.

The way it is set up in the objective world view is this; I have the thought *'I will go to the park.'* I suggest it is my own volitional choice to think that thought (which is the norm of course), and I then undertake that trip. But can I really claim it as my idea? For the fact is that the *impulse* to go to the park arose in an instant, again, it is only

<u>after</u> the impulse arises, that 'I' enter the scene and take ownership of it as 'my idea,' connecting it with other stories and notions presently buzzing around this ever-active intellect. But clearly the thought was not *chosen* from many already present and awaiting selection, it arose – it simply was not ever mine – *I was not even there at the time!*

The concept of my mind, my very identity, simply dissolves without the concept of time. 'I' am a temporal concept, I am simply an idea, a process. As time is a product of mind, mind is likewise a product of time. They are one and the same illusion of continuity. Yet eternity is here and now, and always will be. My eternal nature is ever-present and only seems to be obscured by fascinations of process in time.

Ambiguity

When one looks into a mirror,
it seems as if one is looking at a different object,
And yet one is looking at oneself

Tukaram

Perhaps if the previous argument doesn't satisfy, as it surely will not for any time-mind struggling to protect and maintain its own existence, we could look more specifically at 'where' *within this vessel*, I exist. If it is true that my body houses 'me' then maybe this would bring us closer to finding this elusive character.

This physical vessel is a complex functioning of form appearing to work fairly autonomously with little effort on 'my' part, Its biology seems to work fine without any intellectual interference at all, certainly this is borne out by any infant who miraculously grows and develops quite naturally and spontaneously without intent or personal direction. Likewise with the mind, there seem to be many processes and functions going on continually. For example, we don't *try* to breathe, it is a quite natural functioning of the apparatus. Neither are we intentionally pumping the blood through our veins, orchestrating the velocity of flow, nor directing the operation of the neural networks or maintaining the immune system. No, this all just happens (remarkably) quite naturally and instantaneously. It would be difficult to deny therefore, that life seems to take place within this vessel quite freely and independently of this 'me' character. It is quite a task to find where 'I' figure within all this functioning. Indeed, I may lose a limb, or an ear or an eye or any such appendage, yet my sense of self is not diminished at all.

So, once again I ask where am I in all of this? We are no closer to an answer. Can we, for example, ever really attach any kind of claim as instigator or originator to all of this bodily activity? Is there really a 'John' or 'Jane' at the helm of this unfathomably complex organism that can claim the tiniest involvement in any of these functions as his or her own wilful intent? If, in some way, it is possible that the 'I,' the 'me,' is residing within the brain, surely I could discover this residence? That would seem to be a reasonable investigation. I can certainly agree that if the body should ingest chemical stimulants or undergo some physical trauma, the thoughts and feelings will change as a result of this apparent action. It will indeed seem to behave differently.

Ambiguity

But this brings me no closer to an answer, for irrespective of the type or content of thought or feeling, they remain spontaneous, be they artificially induced delusional thoughts or otherwise. The Brain itself, the cerebral cortex, remains a concept, the very organ that supports this sense of being, is for me right now a concept itself! Even if I should become intimately familiar with the workings of this captain of the central nervous system I would still be no closer to finding 'me' at this present moment. Superior intellectual capacity and academic brilliance affords me no greater access to the immediacy of Self-realisation.

It is perplexing indeed, that all material form is interpreted by the sense organs, which are themselves manifestations of material form. So just how is it possible to prove the tangibility of an objective and independent world of form isolated from idea or concept?

As Robert Powell explains in 'Path Without Form:' " *To establish the Existence of the world, I must first* <u>*assume the existence*</u> *of the world and because the observation system itself is part of the* (manifest) *world, it disproves the notion of a separate, absolute world that can be observed from the point of view of an independent observer.*

So this body, this vessel, is a physical manifestation like any other physical phenomena. Yet not in any real sense *exclusively* 'me,' for it seems to work independently of any volitional involvement. And as thoughts also seem to simply arise (again without 'my' volition) then this mind and body are totally automatic manifestations, yet strangely *I can find no evidence of self in either!*

So could it be that this body and this mind and indeed this world I perceive are ideas arising as spontaneously as any other thought. Should I remove the idea of time, clearly all I would ever have is 'this,' existence, here and now. Form and function as processes of this time-mind, the apparency of my interior mental realm and exterior physical world arising at one and the same instant. It seems that the only accurate thing I can say is that *existence IS, beyond concepts of space and time.*

Both observer and observed, in a material sense, are made of the same stuff, and hence indivisible, observer and observed in unison. There simply is no object-subject environment in truth, only the appearance of such.

Where my identity lies is obviously not dependent upon the actions or behaviours of this physical body, for they change like the wind and arise from the same thought impulse as before. I dance my way through life like a neurotic chameleon changing and adapting my persona for each given situation. There is no constant in all of this change, there is simply no point of anchor or stability to personality. There is merely the ever-running story of life. This story appears hugely complex and involved and includes all the why's and wherefores, the biological history of 'me' and all that entails. My personal history of events and influences, my fears, phobias, loves, likes, dislikes, and all the psychological conditioning that makes up

AMBIGUITY

this idea of 'me'. There is even a global story going on within which my own personal story seem to run. Indeed the multi-dimensional layers and scale of the story can be mind-bogglingly infinite, I can even expand my beliefs to such phenomena as reincarnation for example and now the temporal nature of 'my' life has extended to encompass not only this lifetime but other lives, past and to yet come! Perhaps even different experiences in different worlds. The scope of the adventure in time-mindness is truly fathomless, such is the nature of this amazing temporal phenomenon.

My Temporal Self

Taking oneself to be a person
is a habit just like any other

Jean Klein

So it seems there is one aspect within all of this mental storytelling that would render this whole drama of projection and reflection null and void if it was regarded and observed accurately. What differentiates these stories about 'me' from the present evident reality remains but one concept - time.

These stories are *always* projections in either the direction of past or future. The story's very existence relies upon the belief in this thing called 'time' and links one moment to the next in an apparent flow of mental association.

To illustrate this point lets try another very short and simple exercise:

Stop doing whatever you are doing *right now*, stop thinking whatever you are thinking *right now*. Just stop everything including thinking, just don't do any of it anymore. OK?

What you will obviously and ultimately discover (as with the previous exercise) is that it is quite impossible for what is occurring right now, not to occur, for even an instant. The thoughts that arise do so spontaneously. If it were not so you could rightly claim you were able to stem the flow of thoughts and could do so in any event at any moment.

Now you may claim you *can* indeed do this, but is this really so? For your claim will always be retrospective. Even the claiming itself (if examined accurately) arises only spontaneously, <u>before</u> the *entrance of the claiming entity* – the ego (time-mind). Only upon looking back at the thought does the entity of 'self' appear and claim volition.

The fabrication known as mind exists only in reflection or anticipation, a phantom of time.

All that can be said truthfully and accurately is that in this very instant thoughts arise.

You may have heard the phrase 'as the mind takes me' which is fascinatingly and literally correct. The mind does *take you*, indeed it *makes you*. The mind invents *you as a separate self in time*, you become *it*, as it becomes you, it is a partnership of illusion! Yet in reality nothing exists in isolation to anything else. All is given birth in timeless being.

If you are indeed the volitional captain of the mind then it would be the easiest task in the world to turn your attention to only joyous and pleasurable thoughts, as many self-help proclamations suggest. You could say goodbye once and for all to any negativity. Banish stress, anxiety and worry permanently, simply and profoundly because you *are* the mind, in full and complete control and therefore directing operations swiftly, appropriately, diligently and harmoniously, Halleluiah!

Clearly if this were the case the swelling ranks of psychotherapy services would never see the light of day, and the above exercise would have been a complete doddle. No longer would I stub my toe on that door frame, miss the 9:30 train to Liverpool or have a cross word with my loved ones. All would be perfect sweetness and light because 'I' turn 'my' attention to unreserved joy, period. I select each and every thought and concept throughout each and every moment – ah simple!

Yet even the most disciplined eastern yogi's who can stem the flow of blow to a bodily injury or suffer hours of what most westerners would consider intolerable pain, are merely appearances in space-time. Volition, is simply an appearance. Choice is always secondary – a temporal phenomenon.

The whole idea of claiming is a false one. The instigator of the action is a phantom, there is no personal author. Only ever within that retrospective or anticipatory sense does the attachment of this 'claiming entity' arise. Only *after* a thought has spontaneous arisen is there then a claim of it being 'mine.' Without this mysterious element we call time 'I' no longer have claim to any action be it physical or mental. In fact remove time as a concept and 'I' too completely disappear. There is only ever present spontaneous awareness, or consciousness. The seeming pain and struggle of life is directly proportional to this false association of self as the claiming entity. Once thoughts are observed independently, arising naturally, then is there a gap, a possibility for a 'peace beyond appearance' to enter. But only once the clinging and grasping is no longer exclusively cherished. If I observe, simply look at the *desire to become* anything other than what is present right now, If there is free unattached observation, free from need, ambition and desire, then that detached observation is the key to a deep peacefulness not dependent upon the material manifestation. The appearance is seen in its true light – an arising of form and function.

It is a realisation of the non-specific nature of life. In which we come to see that time is where all fiction begins; where all stories originate, where all confusion is given birth – Time is the only place guilt and anxiety ever has existence.

Time is merely a construct of a wholly false perception.

My Temporal Self

If we absent the concept of a linear progression, despite it's seeming reality, all we have is a simple awareness Here and now. A functioning of form and thought in this instant. All else is assumption, all else is story telling.

The idea that 'I' have choice is false, a misconception. There is no volition in what occurs *right now*. There is only the appearance of choice *after the event*.

In this very instant there is the reading of these words and all the associated mental activity necessary to do so, but all is occurring totally spontaneously within present awareness – Nothing more. 'You' can only claim to read the words after they have been read. *There is*, In fact, only the reading taking place. Look at this deeply – There is only reading happening right now.

Now you may reasonably argue that you can turn away from these words, you can listen to some music, cook an apple pie or choose from any number of activities and turn your mind to equally as many topics. But *you* simply cannot (and never did) do this. Alternative actions will occur of course, any of these things may arise, but only *after* the originating impulse to act. Then and only then, after it's appearance does the claiming entity, the ego, raise its head; only then does this 'me' stake its claim as the doer and orchestrator of all. In truth 'I' cannot go to the park, the going to the park arises. An impulse appears and it is followed. Nobody truly *does* anything, it is simply done, in the moment. Life happens.

Pretend Personality

One is called "Ocean"
The other Called "Ganges"
And though these are different names
Their waters are still the same.

Jnaneshwar

The 'you' that you think yourself to be is a product of time; your very sense of identity is nothing but a temporal illusion, a concept borne of memory and anticipation, an assumption of continuity or linking of past and future events, forming a linear chain in which the life story may unfold. This is a totally automatic phenomena, it is not a chosen course nor a volitional construct as such. But remove the concept of time, this mental construct, and you have to remove the identity that is claimed and the story that was constructed therein. What is left is 'this.' That is all that can be said with any accuracy or validity. It is simplicity itself, this is why it is so easily overlooked, because it is simply not seen.

This personal doer turns to dust in the light of immediate seeing or plain unadulterated observation. The story and what you thought you were is merely a collection of memories, artificially joined to form a fabrication of recollection and association. That's who you believe yourself to be, a make-believe ego - a pretend personality created by time.

The mind retrospectively assesses and connects events and circumstances in a supposedly coherent and orderly fashion, this is the dreamweaver mind, associating and structuring the elements of the story to fit the pattern of the play. The fabric and the pattern of the story enchant and intoxicate, and become the exclusive fascination in which the personality is formed and immersed.

Seeing with clarity that there was, and never could be, an isolated personal doer or author present in any moment, reveals that there is simply whatever is arising presently, nothing more, nothing less. There is real freedom in seeing this, in simply allowing this natural state of unicity of being. But just how this allowing or seeing could arise without choice is the perplexing thing, it will be experienced or otherwise as life will have it and there is nothing and no-one to do anything about it.

For clarity is beyond choice or intention, it is simply the seeing of appearance as it is. The idea that with clarity comes some behavioural change of a loving and benevolent nature is a misconception borne of a dualistic approach. Clarity, observation, is by nature unconcerned with the action in a relational sense. It is clarity that dissolves the relational dialogue altogether.

The mind is apt to jump in at this juncture and demand to know *how* to do this; how to procure this 'state,' how to grasp and obtain this understanding for it's own use. But there is no prescription, no activity that will ever lead to what is already in evidence, beyond intellectual interpretation. All that can be done is to see the obviousness of this present moment, to observe the thoughts arising, to observe the questions, the stories, the pondering, the belief, the disbelief, the angst, the worry, the anticipation and all the many colours and moods of this fascinating thought flow. And yet, who could do this within the grand spontaneity of life?

Within this observation it could be said that the mind is turned against itself in a paradoxical fashion. It is the proverbial removal of the thorn with a thorn. For it can become a fascinating process to watch the mania and compulsiveness of the conditioned mind. It can be a wonderful habit to form, offering a peace which is immediate and liberating. It is what some eastern mystics have termed the 'choiceless witness.'

But there's no question that self-observation can seem a daunting and somewhat bizarre prospect to a mind wholly entrenched in character play. All that hypnotic and melodramatic game playing, though intriguing, can seem to form an inflexible objective barrier to the obvious state of things. But lets be clear, there is no right or wrong in all of this, there is no prescriptive action to adopt, what will be, will be. The story will run as it will, the only question is whether the story is recognised as a drama or believed unquestioningly and consequently lived as a dualistic reality.

For the end of belief in story telling represents the end of time and the end of the exclusive personal perspective. It is the absolute end to right and wrong, judgement and assessment in favour of simple liberating observation.

Everything that was, is and ever could be, is contained within this present moment.

This simple observation may seem like the giving up of everything, yet there is never any loss in all of creation. All that occurs is a correction of view – what was thought to be so, is seen as merely an image, an illusion. The 'me' that dissolves into presence is clearly nothing more than a collection of ideas that only have validity in a relational context, in other words, what I claim as myself, as my individual identity, is actually based entirely upon a relationship to an external objectified world.

To be *'in the world but not of it'* is what we are speaking of here. To live within this liberation is to celebrate life *as it is,* to live freely in the moment - life for life's sake without need to coerce, cajole or strive. But to live in the story as it arises. To truly 'need' nothing and to recognise everything as a whole. Consciousness dancing in form.

Pretend Personality

The moment a step is taken to alter or change behaviour or action *in anticipation of a projected future benefit*, it is a step taken away from present being, present perfection. There is no doer, only action in perfect being.

So what is being suggested is not that the personality is far less than it thinks itself to be, but rather that it arises from the entirety of life, of being. It is an identification with a separate body-mind and a wholly false identification of limitation within a contextual world, which itself arises in timeless being. This vessel, this vehicle of experience can only truly be enjoyed with carefree abandon once it is aware of that which gives rise to it, that which is it's life and existence, that which is at the hear of it's very being.

You are not a singular character within the drama, you are the source and entirety of being.

The Delusion of Division

"Only in quiet waters do things mirror themselves undistorted. Only in a quiet mind is adequate perception of the world."

Hans Margolius

The agitation of the mind and it's continual commentary on events plays out in the apparent span of time, yet time itself is nothing more than a mental association of events into a linear framework, but always *presently* projected within this moment, right now. When feelings of desire, anticipation or reflection are observed clearly they can be seen only as arising as part and parcel of *this present awareness,* despite the resolution of unease seeming to lie within the past or future. The temporal mind story can only ever arise spontaneously *right now, in this moment*, this is all there ever is.

As an example, the fascinating story of enlightenment talked of earlier, can seem to hold future promise from a present state seen as lacking or deficient in some way. The projection or story in this case is one of ultimate attainment, one that will bring continuous bliss or peace, achieved through various paths and processes. In projecting this goal in time, the time-mind places an illusory fence between itself (or rather it's idea of itself) and this future enlightened 'state' it would seek to reach. This self-deception alone creates the longing for what is in fact, already present. There is simply an idea that something is missing, be it knowledge, wisdom or peace. This sense of lack itself creates an agitation or movement to seek, to discover, to figure out and to achieve, and of course, all these things the active mind loves to do. The stories of the time-mind were made for discovery, for seeking, questioning and formulating, for assessing, pondering and evaluating. Yet in all this activity there is absolutely no meaning, though a counterfeit wisdom may be claimed. What does remain however, is considerable guilt, fear and tension and agitation.

There simply is no fence between beingness and itself, like all constructions of mind it is a fabrication of fantasy. The fence is an artificial division. The time-mind *is* personality, a construct of a false sense of self using this fence of individuality to protect it's own existence and identity in a projection of continuity of the life story. Holding itself separate and detached in time from a seemingly illusive state of being, perpetuating the process of self creation in a seeming continuum. Yet the only true defence is to literally remove the idea of this fence or to 'de-fence,' as it were, by present observation of all these constructed concepts and confusions of the mind. Then is there the real possibility that the fence will be seen as nothing more than an attempt to mask what is always present – awareness, here and now. For if God or Source be Eternal, then certainly the Eternal includes this very moment, and if Infinite, then *right here* would equally fall within that definition.

Of course the personality, who you think you are, is fine. Ultimately nothing has been lost in this dream of individual experience, The personality is simply a bag of conditions, a cloak of characterisation and separation that is worn to play this game of human existence. Yet simple present observation can reveal how things really are. If it is seen that right now what is occurring is occurring free of any labelling or secondary narrative, and if we can resist the temptation to identify with those divisional mental commentaries that are continuously running – the ever-chuntering polarised narrative, it becomes patently clear that there is no doer, no author, no volitional action whatsoever, only a natural sense of being, in which everything is happening here and now. And there is nothing wrong or out of place in all of it, for it simply arises in its entirety totally spontaneously. It is only the fabricated time-mind that looks back to evaluate, to question, to judge, And ultimately to form this continuum of division and separation of what is actually a wholly undivided silence.

BEYOND BELIEF

Time gives birth to both judge and jury

A*nything* can seem to happen in this play of life, however, the content of this awareness is extraordinarily infinite. What exists right now is the potential for all things, all events – it is what you are; unlimited potential in expression. But this personal expression, the self-identity, in adopting this limited mental aspect, sees itself separate and isolated from an external or 'outside' world and as such the subject-object relationship seems to arise.

Yet all there really is, is simply the potential for all things within an infinite and whole awareness. The story in which the arising of this separate reactive personality exists, is the nature, construct and reason for the play of life. If there ever was a meaning of life then this is it; For life is its own purpose and meaning. Beneath the wave and ripple of experience lies an oceanic silence of all encompassing beauty and magnitude.

Aspirations and Evaluations

Whoever knows that the mind is a fiction and devoid of anything real knows that his own mind neither exists nor doesn't exist

Bodhidharma,

A psychological evaluation or examination of the personality from an objective point of view, may uncover the workings and tendencies of a particular conditioned-mind within a particular life story. It may be that there is a scenario of depression, of persecution, of liberation or righteousness, or indeed any number of mental fabrications and narratives which seem real and tangible, and indeed within their own realm of experience this will seem so. But what remains constant within all of these mental machinations is absolute presence - The awareness of life in expression presently occurring or conscious awareness; Beingness is dancing it's dance of form.

The moment a sense of 'me' enters the equation an evaluation story takes root and seeks to further establish the reality and validity of it's false perspective.

The desire for an enhanced self-image, sense of self or situation, is locked into the idea of present lack, just as evaluation is the retrospective analysis of past events which further establish this sense of deficiency, in the hope of a future discovery improvement or change. But all attempt at change is grounded in illusion. Being is not a state to be improved upon, completeness is being, as being is complete, whole and eternal. The ambitious mind is blind to this fact. It is locked into levels of assessment, of degrees and improvements, a better/worse perspective which comes with the territory of dualism.

The perceived change of circumstances which arise for a character which seems to feel benefit from an intervention of a psychoanalytical nature (or any other intervention within a life story for that matter) is not 'wrong' therefore, it is simply yet another construct of the drama of life. All that has occurred is that the story has seemed to change. I will borrow the analogy of the kaleidoscope – Changing the coloured shapes into a different order or array offers a different appearance only, it does not reveal the fundamental nature of the kaleidoscope itself.

The analysis of the workings of the character therefore, is further fantasy offering further continuation and substantiation of the narrative, a dream within a dream if you will. The unconditioned will not be discovered *within* the conditioned but only upon recognition of the state of limitation, a discovery beyond volition. It is simply a question of belief; is the story true and seen as reality or is it recognised for the imagery that it really is? All aspects are contained within one whole and complete awareness. There is either unicity or duality.

It may often seem to be the case that when things get really tough, when personal anguish or sadness become heightened, or maybe even through acute inquisitiveness, that the mind turns upon itself and is then drawn to examine these questions of an existential nature: 'Where is this 'self,' 'What is life all about,' 'What is the meaning to all of this?' This longing to know the answers to the big questions, this seeking arises from this sense that actually something isn't quite right - a sense of lack. It is what Buddhists term 'Duka' or uneasiness – a sense that something somewhere is somehow out of place.

This unease which is paradoxically at the root of the idea of individuality, is often the key that opens the door to the examination of the nature of that self, to the discovery of the nature of the fictitious characterisation and consequently the true nature of being beyond appearances.

However, the time-mind is exclusively engaged upon grasping, through aspirations of future grandeur or projected peace in a totally fabricated story. Hand in hand with this projection goes the ever-present evaluative, and consequently judgmental processes, within which the agitated time-mind assesses, contemplates, dissects and arrives at it's all important and resultant path upon which it treads with forthright vigour and determination, to a goal that will shift ever-distant. This is the nature of temporal existence; experience after experience. What is not seen is that this is IT! *This* is the goal, this is the destination, it always was and always will be just THIS. There never was anywhere to *GET TO*.

This is the flawed vision of the time-mind; an imagined blindness which equates to failing to see the wood for the trees. Yet even this apparent avoidance of Self is the perfection of the present arising of awareness, and is wholly complete. This is the great paradox of existence – it cannot be escaped!

The Particular Perspective

The sage does not go, yet he knows
He does not look, yet he sees,
He does not do, yet all is done.

Tao Te Ching

So just what is the value of this knowledge of the true nature of Being? Well, ultimately there is no value whatsoever in mental accumulation of concepts for beingness is always whole and complete. But if it is seen that longing and suffering and the identification with this personal egoic self and all its conditionings are linked, perhaps a more expansive awareness may take root. More simply – 'I' seem to suffer through ignorance of reality. The personality will always seek an improved situation, the horizon always beckons full of promise. This is because the personality – the time mind is a creature of temporality and operates through this limited capacity.

Yet there is nothing inherently wrong with the personality and all its foibles, when it is seen for what it is – simply a characteristic of a dualistic world view. This knowledge however, can offer liberation, a freedom to live life freely, to see thoughts for what they are – a free flowing stream - to allow all to be as it is arising right now, to notice the joyousness of being without condition.

To neither exercise effort nor relinquish the need for effort in a projected process of becoming, but to simply be present to all that occurs, be it anger, elation or anything in between. The actions, the animation is totally irrelevant, truly irrelevant, and in seeing this lies true freedom from the dictates of the story.

But this presence cannot be attained, it is a simple seeing of life in its entirety, the opposing poles once seen as reality are now recognised as the stuff of phenomenal life. Beyond, and yet within this polarised stance itself, stands the invitation of the expansive perspective of the whole. There may still be a preference and desire, but crucially *peace is not dependent upon them.* Peace is present and immediate and from this position all is a joyous delight of form and function. Tension only arises from maintaining a polarised stance – in trying to get somewhere from somewhere else.

How the story of this life evolves is actually quite meaningless from this absolute perspective, other than for experiential purposes; the deep association with the experiencer is the distraction from the obvious nature of the way things really are.

The Particular Perspective

If I remain exclusively attached to this **E**goic-**P**ersonally-**I**dentified-**C**reature, the pain can seem **EPIC** indeed, I can be so entranced with my involvement in this life drama, I have identified myself with this character so completely that the true limitless background from which it arises has been overlooked – bamboozled by the division and complexity of the drama – 'Dazzled by the darkness.' But my true and limitless nature hasn't miraculously disappeared or been dissolved in my 'exodus from Eden,' indeed there are no deeply hidden secrets to cunningly uncover that will avail reality. No, it will simply be noticed or otherwise, arising naturally and spontaneously in each and every moment, or remain obscured by drama and personal involvement. Neither has more virtue than the other.

There is no hierarchy in being.

This enchanting and hypnotic life story will be believed in exclusivity, or it will not. Yet all existential questions of 'why' or 'how,' of beginnings and endings, of meanings and purpose are equally part and parcel of the same belief in temporal existence - in belief in character and circumstance as separate and meaningful. But beingness or presence, like a circle, like a dance, has no beginning or end *it simply is*. But the ever-inquisitive analytical time-mind does not hold to this statement, it has nothing to grasp onto, nothing by which to validate itself, and validate itself it must in order to remain the captain of this temporal vessel.

It is only from this particular perspective of one thing in *relation* to another, that life can seem to be lacking, that there can be a sense that somehow, somewhere something is not quite right; that perhaps something is missing; that something should be done, some effort made to reconcile this lack of equanimity. This is the fundamental nature and seeming plight of the seeker in duality.

The diver only discovers pearls because of the weights which hold him submerged

Richter

The traditional Buddhist story highlights this point; Only upon recognition of the nature of his temporal vessel (the body), and the apparent unavoidable temporality, suffering and sure demise of its biology, was the Buddha's passionate quest for illumination ignited. The sincere hunger to know what lay behind the appearance of the body which was seemingly doomed to degeneration and ultimate death, was the trigger to 'seek' the true reality beyond the temporal appearances. (The discovery upon which, it should be noted, there was great amusement). Oh, and just in case it escapes the mind reading these words, it should be reminded that the story of the Buddha, Jesus Christ, Mohammed, Krishna et al, are likewise all stories happening within the mind - *right now!*

The Particular Perspective

The perpetual seeker, the time-mind, being concept itself, begets further concept by way of evaluation, assessment, projection and reflection. Always these concepts are promoted as beneficial or preferential standards by which to behave or conduct itself. This is pure fantasy however, (spontaneously arising, of course). As an example, money seems to be a considerable issue in the narrative of the western world, this story entails all kinds of attachments and formulae for wealth creation. Equally as potent is the polar opposite of 'moral' resistance and indignation to great financial accumulation – the denial of wealth. But once again, all that is being promoted in either one of these views is a *particular perspective*. Fairness and equal share as a moral stance, has at it's base a concept of right and wrong – a dualistic stance of particular preference - There simply is no such stance, no such moral code outside of the particularised concept of it. There is absolutely no virtue in poverty or lack, and equally none in affluence and abundance. There is simply no factual basis for anything, be it historical reference (present reflection within the story) or material evidence (manifestation of concept). The conditioned individual time-mind will of course argue otherwise, lambasting it's own creation and consequently shooting itself in the metaphorical foot, as it were.

Health of the body organism is another equally charged and emotive subject, being regarded by the time-mind as the source and substance of life itself, rather than the materialised reflection of it. Seen and held in this regard, every measure is taken to continue the body's existence at all costs, despite what can often be seen as very painful and substantially less-than-perfect circumstances. The body is 'aided' to remain functioning at all costs, as longevity presides over quality in this present story, again from the particular perspective.

Seeing through the story itself, seeing beyond beliefs or conditionings will not necessarily alter the apparent material circumstances of life, who knows? There may be vast and substantial change, but all those considerations are irrelevant, mere background considerations, for what disappears or is seen through is the very one who would comment, have investment in opinion upon those changes.

Within the ever-present background of pure being, change is observed without attachment, there is no choice, no desire to fulfill, but simply nonchalant seeing, where nothing need, or could be added. It is a subtle but totally radical shift of perception that may occur or may not. But there is no longer any need to fulfill, but rather the opportunity to do so without any kind of attachment to outcome. Even the particular perspective is simply accepted as a perfect spontaneous arising, a mere functioning of a polarised narrative

However, a character in a movie that was unable to detach from the dramatisation could find it pretty uncomfortable at times, especially when respite was sought. Only If there was awareness of the source which gave life to the whole drama, set, stage, characters and all, could the whole experience be a enjoyed simply for what it was – the drama unfolding. Fully engaging and enjoyable for its own sake, just as a work of art is.

The Particular Perspective

"Be as a child to enter the kingdom of heaven"

A child that plays with gay abandon takes life far less seriously. An infant who's only concern is just how much enjoyment he will get from whatever he is doing with little or no concern for past or future, a child is this fully playful mode (or indeed an adult for that matter) has this *quality* of carefreeness, a childishness that is a most peculiarly rich state of mindlessness. When we are fully engrossed in the enjoyment of our activities, we no longer have a commentary playing but are fully present in our actions, fully alive. Perhaps you have heard the phrase: " *I was lost in the moment*." Never was a truer phrase spoken; the 'I,' the particular, the idea of 'me' was absent in the doing, in the action; dissolved by pure present enjoyment; revealing the truth and simplicity of *here and now*, whole and complete, without the persistent commentary that always takes the attention anywhere *but* the present moment.

In this joy of timeless being is the temporal voice of anticipation, guilt and desire is laid to rest, the chattering tyrant simply cannot survive the power of presence. Nor indeed can the voice of fear, another of the painful masks worn by the tempestuous time-mind. The clarity that comes from recognising and seeing these mental superimpositions for what they are, is highly amusing, to no-one!

All those 'shoulds,' could haves' and maybes' can then be seen for what they are - the demanding ranting of the manic time-mind, the impostor that would hold freedom hostage to past behaviour and future action. The moment there is awareness of this commentary, this ever-present overlay of dialogue, there comes detachment from another strand of the rope of persistent self-analysis.

The particular perspective of the time-mind is both judge and executioner, passing sentence and condemning present peace to temporal oblivion. When the character is unmasked however, life can be enjoyed fully and freely – *as the play it is*. It's not about loosing the character as such, but fully observing and delighting in it's being, only the observer can avail of this recognition.

Of course you will do as you will do – actions and words will spontaneously arise as they ever did, despite what this text may or may not suggest. But once Being is simply recognised as it is - the journey of life is seen in it's true context – not a finite journey of limited distance at all, but an eternal dance; The dance of infinite expression.

Death of Future Promise

*Look at your expectations of tomorrow and
you expose your beliefs about you today.*

Himal (Michael J. Hadfield)

There is then a direct correlation between this lack of awareness of true being and the degree to which one is invested in the drama of personal life. In other words the more one detaches from personal goal orientation, from the struggle and striving to attain and grasp results in time, from the invitation of future promise, the more a sense of peace or freedom may flourish. It is within this allowing, this unconditional flowing of life that freedom truly exists. Rather like a parent's love for his child, a love that arises without reason, prompting or deliberation; a love that is simply a profound yet extraordinarily powerful love that arises miraculously, quite naturally and spontaneously. It is yet another paradox - an awareness that is both simple and extraordinary. An ever-available state of being, (which actually is beyond a 'state' as such) and needs only recognition which comes from the lowering of the volume of the seemingly persistent chatter of the egoic grasping mind. This can only be done by recognition – seeing things as they are – honest natural observation. In truth nobody can do this at all – it will arise or otherwise. All that can be seen is the misleading narrative of the time-mind's persistent promise.

Once seen, the chasing of the rainbow no longer holds the promise of gold. There is the realisation that the crock of gold is immediate, forever lying under one's feet, no matter where you seem to wander you are unavoidably within the rainbow. The ego is the proverbial beggar aloft the chest of unfathomable treasure, unaware of it's eternal presence.

There is no necessity for change, to make an effort, to alter actions or behaviour in order for this awareness to arise, though change is part and parcel of temporal existence. Those who would seek to improve the self *in order to gain* a glimpse of a state of non-self, peddle in delusion. For only within the story is future promise dependent on behavioural deeds, only the character lost in his own action of characterisation chases phantoms and promises.

There is only one way - seeing through the drama - recognising the story for what it is, nothing more is, could or ever was needed. There is simply no need to remain duped by the false promises of time that place your happiness in the next relationship, the next pay check, the very next day, or indeed salvation and deliverance after bodily death.

DEATH OF FUTURE PROMISE

Your happiness lies where it has forever existed, *here and now* awaiting its simple recognition in timeless being. Beyond behaviour, beyond belief.

The play is not going to change - nothing is going to get better or worse - but what emerges is the one that sees. Clear seeing is simply seeing without anyone being there.

Tony Parsons

The delusion of the time-mind narrative speaks counter to this wisdom. It instigates the chase undertaken by the seeker, along with the perpetual grasping, the studying and striving for what seems to be elusive, and yet each step taken in time is a step away from *that which is already present*. In truth their simply is 'no one' who can step away from the inherent nature of being, but the stronger the pull of imagined future promise, the louder the voice for achievement rings. Yet the calm waters of present being remain undisturbed by this delusion, despite the attention being turned to time and its illusory promise.

When you look into yourself nakedly
there is only this pure observing,
there is a lucid clarity without anyone being
there who is the observer;
only a naked manifest awareness is present.

Beyond Belief

This awareness is empty and immaculately pure, not being
created by anything whatsoever.
It is authentic and unadulterated, without any duality.
Clarity and emptiness.
This inherent self-awareness does not derive
from anything outside itself.
This is the real introduction to the actual condition of things.

(Padmasambhava)

Nothing changes once the sense of individuality is seen through, the illusion of separate parts is seen as this - an illusion of subject/object that never existed at all. But the minds necessity to seek change or improvement in some way is part and parcel of the play of life in time. The idea that when 'I' become 'enlightened' everything will be different *for me* is simply not so. In fact the common reaction to a realisation of the true nature of self is laughter! Pure delight at the simplicity of way things really are. A realisation that this 'me' was pure fiction, total conjecture based upon a false connection of events, with all the angst and drama so heavily invested in, forming the texture or flavour of the drama.

Change is simply not a characteristic of absolute being. Appearances however are rooted in change. The character will seem to alter within the drama, conditioned as it may be within the narrative, but there is fundamentally a recognition of the true context and relationship of the true self to the character. (although truly one and the same). Motives for actions will still arise, but crucially the disturbance or movement of mind is seen as simply the functioning of form, it need not change necessarily, it will be experienced as all experiential states are, but without the tension or anxiety arising from attachment to the outcome or the sense of volitional involvement.

Does this mean one becomes a passionless automaton oblivious to life and no longer interacting in an experiential manner? (there is no 'one' of course) Quite the contrary, Absolutely not. For now experience is free of tension and can be enjoy wholeheartedly in each and every moment, free of the angst of striving for a 'better' situation, free of the guilt of reflecting actions and behaviour for it is all seen and lived *right now* absent of secondary commentary. This is illustrated perfectly in the maxim *"All paths lead nowhere, so choose a path with Heart!"* Conversely, there is the story of the Zen Monk Banzan, who whilst walking in the marketplace overheard the conversation between a butcher and his customer. " *Give me the best piece of meat you have"* said the customer. To which the butcher replied, *"but everything in my shop is the best."* The story goes that the monk was instantly realized upon hearing this.

So simple present awareness is a recognition that there is not a better or indeed worse state in truth. Nor is the ego an entity or character separate from the play itself, but the player – the character is intrinsically an appearance within, and in no way isolated from, the entire play unfolding naturally. Nothing has changed about the story of 'my life', the story and the characters are afforded the same freedom to act as they will – an appearance is an appearance is an appearance – meaningless, but fascinating and truly enjoyable. If an impulse to act in a certain way arises then it will be followed as before. If there is an impulse to eat a certain type of food for example, then that will be followed. There is simply no longer a necessity to alter or change anything, but as change and alteration occur and arise, then so shall it be. There is simply no longer any resistance to life, but a free flow of observation within which the action arises.

It is a fundamental shift from Goal orientation to present awareness. In the former peace is ever-promised, in the latter it is ever-present.

The whole temporal aspect of living, the anticipation and expectancy no longer has the same pull or potency, once this has evaporated the unfolding of the life story is observed naturally and spontaneously happening. Without the secondary judgemental commentary upon the action, berating the behaviour of self and that of others, as they are all clearly seen as the entirety of life in motion. There is simply no need for anything to be other than it is, there is peace and enjoyment, there is no longer any fraught tension, guilt or desire. The character has been unmasked, and though it may act in the same characteristic fashions and has many of the same neuroses, tendencies and preferences, crucially this is now totally allowable and acknowledged for what it is; the appearance arising within present awareness. The play, the player and all other characters, simply aspects of the same phenomena. Now this anger can arise without guilt. Now this embarrassment can arise without feeling undermined and now fears and phobias can bee seen as what they are – NOTHING! It is only upon watching the stories of the mind that suddenly, somehow there seems to be an observer; there seems to be something, some presence that observers without attachment, that simply sees and is completely nonchalant to the whole cacophony of form and function. At first it seems to come and go, drifting in and out of the involvement, yet once seen it always remains, inviting it's own recognition so to speak. It's simple mantra being 'SO WHAT?'

My wife just walked out on me without a word after 15 years of blissful marriage – *So what*? Has peace been altered in the slightest by this? No, not at all.

My Business of 25 years just went bankrupt – *So what*? Has eternal being lost in any of its integrity? No, absolutely not.

I have been diagnosed with terminal illness and have been given only a few months to live – So what? Does eternal being have a lifespan that can be counted by mortal measure, never!

All of these events arise and are endemic of being - of life - arising in all its colourful arrays and patterns, nothing is amiss, nothing is out of place, all is arising quite magnificently in present awareness. All potent and animated reactions to those examples can be as acute as they will be, it is not about an aloofness or a disengagement with life but rather an complete embracing of all.

Of course life throws up dramatic and outwardly devastating events, but in what position is the individual to assess the meaning of it all? This tiny individual perspective gives not a hint of the totality of existence within its own isolation of view.

Temporality is change, the swing of polarities. So let it change! See the character, live life! Let it change, watch it, see the madness, enjoy the mayhem and all the exhilaration from the detached perspective, after all it is ultimately all the same stuff, so why not invite that nonchalant observer and laugh at the whole panorama and pronounce with a wide grin – *So what!*

There may be voices of dissention proclaiming this is not a loving way to behave, but let it be clear that this is not a moralistic proclamation or directive as to acceptable norms of behaviour , but fundamentally a different way of engaging with apparent external appearances. Eternal being is unconditioned by nature, it is beyond opinion or moral codes of conduct. What will be will be, so why not be that proverbial leaf upon the surface of the river of life, let it flow where it will, let all arise as it will, act as you will in the moment – It is all the flow and movement of life arising from eternal being. Watch and enjoy!

Inner knowing of the unconcerned observer sees with clarity that all life is meaningless in terms of achievement. It knows its own integrity and eternal unconditioned being and recognising this sees equally the futility of placing peace in a projection of circumstance.

Perhaps it is more easy now to understand the religious doctrines and wisdoms from this detached perspective. For when we look at statements such as *'The meek shall inherit the earth.'* It is not too big a stretch of the imagination to suggest that the attribute of meekness spoken of in this Biblical reference is not a personal achievement to be attained by correctional behaviour, but rather corresponds to the angst-free state that is so typical of one who has discovered the true nature of self and simply or 'meekly' watches without attachment to outcome, and in the very act of acknowledging or recognising peace where it really is – here and now - inherits all there is, where it truly lies. We could as equally suggest *'Entering the kingdom'* refers likewise to the same state of acceptance.

Likewise when we read the statement *'Judge not, lest yea be judged'* we are apt to jump to the conclusion that this too is a directive – a command which will bring *future* reward if we are somehow able to comply. Yet could it not be interpreted as a simple counterpoint between the ego and ego-less states. Clearly to judge, to proclaim another 'wrong' is an attribute of one who is rooted within the relative narrative of right and wrong, one who sees through conditioned vision, one who sees a threat to his temporal personality, a storyteller's world of judgement and retribution where the story teller mind believes not only in its own story, but also in its moral evaluation of the seemingly separate characters around it (Characteristics which it projects itself).

Hence it binds *itself* within a judgemental relative world of evaluation and conflict not through condemnation of an external Deity, but by its very own hand of confusion

Yet even these moral codes are nothing other than conditionings of a superficial and highly transitory nature. If one is solely grounded within the personality drama there will be a thirst to maintain this false sense of self, to protect this temporal ego. In seeing a threatening world the time-mind takes its stand and with iron fist gripping tightly it's treasured beliefs, insisting upon its claim to a righteousness based entirely upon fiction.

Judgement is purely of the time-mind, the personality. Eternal being is wholly without judgement. It is unconditioned and therefore not a selective process at all, being wholly complete and without opposite or opposition. To '*Judge not*' therefore, is simply, but profoundly, a declaration of insight and wisdom, a statement that the state of mind in time is truly unable to judge from it's conditioned perspective. But should it do so, then it will see the fruits of that judgment in a world that isolates and mirrors it's own condition.

The Spiritual Journey

Keep your heart clear and transparent
And you will never be bound.
A single disturbed thought, though,
Creates ten thousand distractions

Ryokan

The nature of the body mind in time is merely a set of characteristics – a particular expression. There is nothing wrong with this functioning organism, nothing to be fought against or discarded, disregarded or abandoned. The conditioned self is a functioning of relative existence and as such operates within an apparent time frame with a specific outlook, with influences of race, culture, geography, society and genealogy to name but a few, yet with many other aspects colouring it's temporal identity.

To fight against this identity is merely to create another temporal story within the already existing paradigm of change. Irrespective of the nature of the story of the individual, this apparent individual can be seen or observed as simply the perfect functioning of existence within a temporal setting. *The key is not effort to change it nature*, but simple seeing. It is neither effort nor the relinquishment of effort, for there simply is, by definition, no volitional action that could ever reveal the reality that totally destroys the very concept of an independent 'instigator of action.'

The secondary dialogue of mind which demands that things should have worked out differently, that insist upon corrective actions or behaviours – this is the impostor. The mind that identifies itself as the author and orchestrator of the action. The chain of though which, given licence, will seek to chase phantoms. The same thought stream which places satisfaction in future or in recalled moments.

There is absolutely no way of 'achieving' this awareness, no action to be taken, no path to follow, for the first step taken toward this projected goal is the first step of denial of its present existence. There is absolutely no prerequisite for present being, no loving action ,no surrendered state, no renunciation and most certainly no holy scripture with which to adhere – none or any of these disciplines may lead to pure present revelation, there is no prescription. What 'this' is, is totally without definition, it is clarity and presence which is ever-present and may only seem to be avoided.

The Spiritual Journey

The human condition however, reinterprets this avoidance of self as a quest, a journeying and a seeking. This gives rise to the idea of 'spirituality' separate from present being. *No such division exists.* One cannot be more or less spiritual, these are simply human misconceptions which entice the mind to further searching and 'deeper' discovery, all of which are it's life blood and upon which its thrives.

This is perhaps one of the most subtle and convincing stories of all – that the key to 'my awakening' lies in my own hands! This is the myth and ultimate deception of the spiritual quest. Not that is *impossible*, but rather that there is <u>somebody who has the ability to achieve it</u>. Once again another story (and a rather cunning one at that) is being spun by the time-mind. It is the age old story of attainment but in a different disguise. Yet there simply is nowhere to get to, no future level to reach, no hierarchy, no discipline to master, and why? Because this is once again pure projection! A story of promise – of becoming – of improving – of change. It is the overlooking of the present in which all is contained.

There is an absolutely certain way to determine whether the mind is peddling a story or not – and that is to ask this one very simple question: '*Where does this place my peace or happiness?*' If the answer lies anywhere *other than here and now*, you can be assured that it is the rambling promise of the storytelling time-mind.

The Spiritual quest is clearly a promise of future bliss, another self-deception or avoidance of what is already present and complete. For a quest is only relevant if something is sought that is assumed *not* to be present already, and this is not the case in reality, awakening is the simple recognition of what is already awake.

Spiritual searching, as with all other forms of questing, is fine, they are part and parcel of the story and fabric of existence. The story is fine in whatever form it takes, whether your role be the martyr or murderer, criminal or cardinal, it makes no difference at all. The only question is do you wish to live in story land alone or be grounded in present awareness? Either is fine but only one a reality.

Earlier we looked to discover where 'I' existed, and found it was difficult to actually pinpoint this 'me' with any degree of certainty. Equally it could be argued that when we embark upon such endeavours as becoming 'more spiritual' we are declaring quite the opposite to our earlier evaluation – In fact we are stating that we *fundamentally believe* in this material vessel as the root of our being. Furthermore, having accepted this fallacy we are now going to embark upon disproving it! And no doubt in some future ceremony or ritual we will indeed discover ourselves or 'awaken.' But not Here, and never Now – that would be just a little too simple!

As A Course in Miracles aptly states the mantra of the ego (time-mind) is '*seek, but do not find.*' All these elaborate deceptions are simply smokescreens to what already exists. The ultimate avoidance of now.

Now is the only item on the
menu of existence.

Resistance

*The heart is peaceful and joyful when we
no longer imagine that we need something*

Eric Baret

There are aspects within the story of life that can seem to offer pointers to awareness, or lack of it. One of these is resistance. In any life situation it is fair to say that the greater the feeling of disturbance or resistance, the greater the investment with the character and to particular outcomes. In other words the greater the goal orientation and the need for a particular, polarised result the more suffering is felt when these needs or desires are not met.

You will perhaps have heard the phrase: '*Real freedom comes not from having what you want, but wanting what you have.*' Resistance is our own in-built desire monitor, letting us know just how invested we are in having what we want, revealing just how strongly we are listening, and believing the storytelling mind. It is a reaction to what is, to what is present.

Resistance is a keen tool in the hands of awareness.

So can we make an effort to become more aware? Well, Actually, no! Effort is rooted in the same imaginary idea of volitional transformation or personal change. The Time-mind will spin many a convincing tale to the contrary and persuade otherwise. But it remains the case that *effort is only made real by the appearance of one who can make that effort* – The Storyteller – the personality – the time-mind.

The person, the individual, the ego, is but an object of perception, it is only by habit or error that we identify ourselves with our perceptions and this is itself the cause of all our suffering

Jean Klein

Observation is the key. At some point it will be seen that there is a story running, and simply this alone. Observation, being still, without preference, is not so much an effort as a way of being. One is not 'trying' in any sense to alter or coerce life, but rather watching from a nonchalant detached standpoint, neither hoping, avoiding nor accepting.

Resistance

To the egoic state this may sound like death, giving up, throwing the towel in. The time-mind is locked into investment, into particular outcome, into making better, improving, changing. This may sound like complete lunacy to the material everyday world of attainment. But let us be clear, freedom is a dish wholly untouched by ego, for freedom is the constant undivided silence behind form and function, that which originates every individual action yet encompasses all.

Resistance is a clenched fist holding tightly to desire. Indeed desire and resistance are two sides of one coin. But lest we forget 'all things must pass.' The temporal world is a world of comings and goings, let it come, let it go, your eternal nature is unaffected by change. So enjoy! Enjoy your struggle to meet the mortgage payments, enjoy your hours stuck in that traffic jam, your finding your lover cheating on you, why? Because it is all the self same thing, it means nothing, it is utterly valueless! So enjoy it for what it is. And *so what!*

One does not have to surrender to a life of persecution or capitulate to poverty, hunger or humiliation, to justify one's anger or lack of charity to 'another,' but just as surely as they are avoided are they equally given life and sustenance. Observation is a watcher not a dictator of actions. It is not a creature of preference. Observation is the timeless ground behind all action and opinion. If there be a 'truth' this is the only truth existent. A state beyond opposites. An immeasurable and eternal present awareness encompassing all and accepting of everything as it's own. It is neither inert nor redundant, but the life and source of every impulse ever felt, the ground and source of every discovery every made, the warmth and light of every love affair ever shared. It is the incomprehensible and inconceivable magnitude of being.

Whenever we attack another, it is out of an idea that we are powerless in the face of the situation. The attack, in whatever form it takes, is a demonstration of *a belief* in an inherent individual weakness. It proclaims a belief in our isolation, in our inability to accept the present. Just as our own judgement condemns us to the same prevailing conditions of judgement upon us, so too is attack equally co-sustained. Fear will always attack. Fear is the anticipation of suffering, yet another counterfeit characteristic of the time-mind, sustained only by the concept of vulnerability. Yet this too is the infinite in appearance, dancing the dance of temporal existence upon a polarised canvas.

Acceptance

Make the smallest distinction and
heaven and earth are set infinitely apart

Sosan

To possess wealth of heart is to possess the true and eternal riches untouched by mortal notions of gain, but the sense of personal individuality exists only within polarity, that is, within a realm of duality, pain and pleasure. Indeed this very sense of separateness is maintained by this apparent but constant movement between those polarities. So what then is acceptance In the context spoken of here? It is nothing other than that same observation. One does not have to become detached from life and all that is going on within that life story. However, when there is a detachment from the outcome, from the action and movement of the mind, a spacious awareness, in which acceptance in the true sense appears. Standing at the centre point, the still point and observing the motion whilst being present and active within it.

The appearance of pain and attack, of suffering and anger for example, may result in the body-mind, the entity, performing all kinds of actions, which may be labelled by many adjectives; heroic, passive, lazy, eager, it doesn't really matter which one we use. It is not the action that is at issue here, rather it is the awareness, the seeing, the observing, the detachment.

To live only the relative story-life involves the continual shifting from pain to pleasure identified only with the objective mind. To seek one polarity without the other is a meaningless, futile and ultimately impossible dream.

There is only one route to lasting peace, and that is not a journey at all but the simple observation and embracing of the here and now, to see through the dramatisation of the mind in favour of the stillness from which it all arises.

The more the time-mind story is adopted or accepted in it's polarized stance, the more painful life can seem to become. The less flexible and the more rigid we seem to be, and the greater the liability to breakage.

The time-mind can be a very convincing storyteller and will demand an audience. It will dig its heals in a give gravity and reality to its story of conditioning. It is the creator of depression and all forms of discontent. It is a product of time and as such a child of polarity. It cannot exist outside of a relative domain and will dogmatically insist upon its virtue and reason against an externalised opposition, this is the very fabric of the illusion it creates – *opinion based isolation*. It has a temporal concept that knows nothing of timeless being, it will seek out any avenue that promises stability and reinforcement of its arguments and projections. – It remains however, nothing more than a fascinating illusion, a deception, a polarised story.

There is a delightful passage in *'A Course in Miracles'* that relates this egoic deception to us in this way….

'This is your "enemy"- a frightened mouse that would attack the universe. How likely is it to succeed? Can it be difficult to disregard its feeble squeaks that tell of its omnipotence…… Be not deceived by the illusions it presents of size and thickness, weight, solidity, and firmness of foundation. Yes, to the body's eyes it looks like an enormous solid body, immovable as is a mountain. Yet within you is a force that no illusions can resist.'

Whether the term 'enemy' is appropriate is open to question perhaps, though the passage is clearly symbolically and eloquently illustrative of the nature of the subject matter in question, essentially stating that despite all animated assertions to the contrary an illusion remains an illusion. We remain deceived only by listening and believing a story as the reality.

Life is a Roller Coaster

Every thought and every breath is a breath
and a thought occurring in awareness;
And we are that awareness.

(Mooji)

Imagine you were riding the most magnificent roller coaster ride ever constructed. A enormous complex of awesome and intricate climbs and twists. Imagine that nobody had informed you that it was a fairground ride – an amusement intended for pure enjoyment. What if nobody had told you that it didn't matter how high, how fast, or how absolutely stomach-churningly nauseas the ride became, you were perfectly safe no matter what took place.

How do you think it would it feel to experience the ride as real as opposed to an entertainment? Never knowing if you were headed for immanent death by slamming into the next concrete wall, or being hurled into oblivion atop the next high-rise turn! Just imagine the trepidation of rising higher and higher into the skies, then plummeting at break-neck speed to the darkened depths, and into those white-knuckled twists and turns totally oblivious to what was lying in wait; in the next drop, the next loop the loop, the next descent. For most of us it would be a pretty harrowing experience, if, (*if* mind you), we were unaware of the true nature of the ride - as an intended source of amusement.

But with a different perspective, with a more informed view – armed with the knowledge of the true nature of the ride, we encounter a wholly different experience. Now we are able to enjoy the ride, even thought materially nothing about it has changed. But absent this knowledge, this understanding of what is truly happening and there could well be that continual struggle and striving for safety – albeit a futile struggle.

Indeed, if you believed that there was an imaginary steering wheel in front of you, keeping you in control of the ride, you would no doubt be trying all sorts of tricky manoeuvres to direct your course, only to be left pondering as to why things didn't always seem to go as planned.

This sense of there being something not quite right, this idea that somehow there is something wrong with the ride however, would be wholly based upon the idea that *you* were in control of the carriage. – You aren't and never were! It is this limited perspective that creates all the discomfort.

There's another funny thing about our ride that I must just let you into, and that is the assumption that the best bit, the most enjoyable and rewarding part, the biggest thrill and the surest safety, has either already happened or is just around the next bend, such is the nature of this cosmic roller coaster ride – placing fulfilment always behind or in front of our carriage, anywhere but where it always does reside – right at the point where you always are – right here, right now.

What is fundamentally overlooked is that all the action, every last rattle and shake is absolutely as it should be, there is no need, and actually no possibility, of effecting volitional change in any way. Every bump and jolt, every nerve jangling twist and exhilarating plunge are completely as they should be. The ride is simply to be enjoyed *as it is*. But true enjoyment can *never* arise when it is not experienced where it already exists. Without awareness of the nature of what is really happening in our analogical carriage there will always be a desire for some other condition in some other place or time that holds out the promise of a brighter future. There is no such thing, no such place. Present perfection is here and now, no matter how the mind may twist it's interpretation.

If we are aware of the true nature of the roller coaster ride; that it is perfectly safe and to be enjoyed for enjoyment sake, then now those white-knuckled clenched fists become open-palmed hands waving atop arms stretched high into the air with the immense exhilaration and freedom of expression, now we can ride like the wind with broad smiles and hearts filled with shear joy and pleasure. Yet nothing at all has altered, in terms of the appearance, everything is happening exactly as before - the highs and lows, the twists and turns, the bone-rattling shudders are just the same, yet the *context* in which it is experienced has indeed altered. The tiny voice of the observer has emerged and whispered 'all is well.' And the ride is finally seen in it's correct perspective.

Why Am I here?

Of all the thoughts that arise in the mind, the 'I' thought is the first. It is only after the rise of this that the other thoughts arise.

Sri Ramana Maharshi

'Why am I here?' is the question of the imaginary seeker – Why am I here, this is the fundamental 'error' which leads to all others. This is the question from which all others arise. Every 'why' question is in fact a statement of delusion, which proclaims the phenomenal subject-object existence as the reality and not simply the appearance. Reality does not arise as a result of any pre-condition. Presence is dependent on no- thing, lacking nothing and without error, whole and complete.

It could be said then, that even the questioning 'Why?' that arises in 'error,' is in fact just as whole and perfect *as an appearance* within totality and is a part of the consciousness in which it was sourced. Indeed, and In truth, there are absolutely no accidents, no errors or emissions, there are appearances of thought, manifestations of mind, all of which are wholly appropriate and spontaneous. But for the purposes of debate, this 'why' question is rooted in a belief in a doer of the action or thought. All questions of this nature contain this root assumption of a volitional doer, an entity about, and *to* which, all things happen. There is a particular perspective, again a polarised orientation, a here and a there and of course often the desire to be anywhere but here!

It could be suggested that it is a grand game of hide and seek in which true being seeks to find itself, simultaneously wishing and not wishing to be successful (at the same time). The perpetual cycle of becoming is continually pointing to the nature of itself. All arises out of eternal being, this is what everything is pointing towards. It is a game of forgetfulness and recognition, all arising right now.

There is no finite self of course, and so there is nobody to do anything in a volitional sense, there is no improvement to make, no time in which to do it and nowhere to get to. It would be total contradiction to suggest otherwise. Yet that is exactly what the appearance of life *would* suggest. Herein lies our conundrum, for appearances do contradict the notion of completeness.

All that can be done therefore, is to observe what is occurring. But absent of a volitional doer –a chooser, all that can be said is that this

WHY AM I HERE?

will happen or not, absolutely spontaneously. It is only the appearance in time that gives the illusion of choice.

For example, if a directive was given within these pages as to how one could achieve a particular state, it would seem contradictory, and yet if that were to be offered then it would be wholly appropriate. Such is the nature of this paradox. If there were an outcry or argument ensuing as to the validity, sincerity or appropriateness of the words and suggestions made here it would all be perfectly spontaneous in the grand scheme of things. The phenomenon of life simply arises and falls. Motion and movement, both conflict and agreement making up the tapestry of life; war, peace, love and hate, all dualistic aspects of the same temporal coin.

Acceptance is often sighted as a key to developing awareness, or the oft promoted 'surrendering to what is.' Both terms can be helpful or misleading depending on how they are applied. Observation on the other hand is simply observation. There is no implication as to the correctness or otherwise of observing, there is only the observation.

In observation physical and mental actions of the personal character are not relevant beyond the immediate. Preferences, mannerisms, all the conditionings of the apparent individual's habits and actions will all still arise as part of that character. That's fine. In observation there is a shift of emphasis from the action to the observation itself, this can create a gap between the wholly identified character and the awareness in which the character arises. It may be possible that the spontaneity is recognised. Again it is possible that this can give rise to greater and greater clarity, but there is absolutely no volition or intention (or certainty) in any of this, there is merely a possibility that this could arise, and again this is more storytelling.

In present awareness it is seen that guilt and regret are further aspects of the story, feelings which arise out of an idea that there can be error in either thought or action of the character.

The watching of the story unfolding with no secondary involvement can free the entity from its false mental associations.

Consciousness (beingness) adopts myriad masks in order to play the various roles and scenes within the play. These words arise just as spontaneously as the concept of contradiction does – it is all consciousness flowing in and through life, all totally appropriate and natural. Whatever the role maybe, whatever the appearance, it is absolutely fine – remember there is nothing wrong, there are no mistakes here. There is no requirement for any of it to be different.

Remember also that volitional change is not possible, change will or will not occur, there is no volitional involvement though appearances in time would suggest otherwise.

So the only accurate thing to say is 'lets see' just sit back and enjoy the show and if involvement occurs, so be it, Let it be, if not, so be it. All is well.

In observation there is the possibility that the potency of the mental involvement will simply fall away revealing the magnificently ordinary truth of being.

Why am I Here?

Observation is not opinion however. Observation is neutrality. A detachment, not from the experience that is happening in the present moment, but a detachment from the time-story as the fundamental driving force and meaning. With this quality of choiceless awareness every moment can be lived as an end in itself, full, vibrant and complete. The question of preference, liking or disliking, is no longer the debate, though they may still be present as functions of the play. The actual occurrence is irrelevant - the action is merely the shifting appearance of form, nothing is sought, for nothing is lacking. There may be anger, passion, desire, or any number of feelings and emotions, but all are given birth from the ever-present quality of undisturbed being, the source or no-thing from which all things become.

So just how do we find this origination when the 'one' who would do this is a total fabrication in the first place? There is absolutely no action mental or physical that can be taken that would in anyway free one from the false sense of individuality, for that very action if claimed as volitional, takes place within the play and by the actor within the context of the drama – the story world. Any attempt at 'self-liberation' claimed by the character merely re-establishes that false sense of individual doership, implying that 'I' can do something, take some action in order to recognise the none existence of this one who acts, which is clearly nonsense.

Observation on the other hand is simply observing, if there is no claim or direction of the observation. If there is no attachment to an outcome or result of any kind, but merely a non-resistive 'honest watching' as it were. Then the thoughts and actions that arise may be seen with greater clarity as simply that which is arising. The dualistic pull of preference is diminished, the desire to be other than where one is, is seen also as less attractive and along with that detachment can come a clarity, a welcoming of this very moment as it appears, pain or pleasure melding into one experience, one infinite timeless moment of being.

This is the recognition of timeless being, the character may or may not change, it is actually quite irrelevant as the appearance is always secondary. The awareness in which all appearance arises is not so much returned to, as revealed as never having gone anywhere in the first place. The return is in fact the re-cognition, the re establishment of Truth or Clarity.

To discover that there is no meaning to life outside of present experience, that there is no point to the struggling and striving, can be a very bitter pill to swallow for the time-mind, but such is the outcome of the investment in personal doership or ownership. The storyteller *needs* for there to be a reason to our story, a drive an ambition a goal. It is chasing the rainbow with all it's might, it is tiring, exhausting even, it demands that there must be a pay off in all of this searching!

But even this struggling and striving unite in silent awareness when simply observed, when they are beheld void of attachment.

For life is its own meaning and purpose, experience is the game that can be enjoyed as it is. It is rarely enjoyed when one has one's eyes ever on the horizon, ever overlooking what is present.

Why am I Here?

Let's go back to our roller coaster ride for a moment. There is absolutely no *point* to the ride itself outside of enjoyment, it needs no alteration nor *can* it be altered. The lack of enjoyment is exactly proportional to the sense of there being something wrong or out of place with the ride.

What individual personality seeks is meaning and purpose to all its activities; all it's struggling to right the track must count for something! All anguish and toil to smooth the ride, to stay on the pleasure track and avoid the painful route must surely be rewarded. But always and ever is this seeking awaiting a *future* fulfilment, <u>the one place that can never be found and will never be reached</u> - *for it simply does not exist.*

In the seeking for future release is the imaginary wheel of suffering spun.

The ride has to be recognised as an entertainment, an end in itself, not a means to an end, before the idea of 'no meaning' has any appeal or acceptance. If there is still a heavy involvement or strong attachment with the doer, lost in the drama of characterisation, suffering the anxiety and torment of struggle, then of course there will be the desire for it to mean something, for the investment and desire walk side by side within the drama or personalisation of 'my story.' Indeed the seeking is rooted in a self-image that assumes it can discover something, and in that discovery it can become more of itself, greater, wiser, more virtuous perhaps. But these transitory qualities like grains of sand slip through the fingers of time and are lost forever In the chasm of memory, only to arise once again in a different guise in space-time, ultimately to be consigned to suffer the same fate.

Reflections

A mind ever free of its own process
Beholds the True miracle of Absolute Reality.
A mind ever lost in its own process
Sees only the forms of this world

Tao Te Ching

The time-mind spins its tale whilst all the while being unaware that the fabric of it's story is a reflection of its own state of awareness, being a mirror unto it's own condition.

Being rooted in a sense of incompleteness it projects its fears outward, creating an external enemy that must be guarded against. It is a state of mind that believes it can account for this innate deficiency by gaining and grasping both material and mental advantage in order to fill this void.

Herein lies the world of combat and competition – a reflection of this vulnerable state of mind in fear, confusion and defence. Looking out upon this mirrored world of madness, it proclaims it's own wisdom and builds it armoured fortress of defence, but a defence against what exactly? – against it's own delusion, and thereby justifying its insanity.

The time-mind is a delusional story and nothing more. All stories are simply fragments of the whole taken in isolation. A stream of thought coalescing into form and function, creating worlds upon worlds within it's own awareness, playing each part as though independent of the other in a mirage of materialism. An elaborate pretence that would be amusing were it not lived so seriously.

Any sense of vulnerability is given life by a belief in separate identity.

So this false sense of vulnerability is a result of identification and attachment to this temporal, physical entity that has an apparent limited span of life and seems deteriorate and change within time. Both body and environment do, of course, appear to undergo natural change as a consequence of temporal existence. But this identification with the transitory creates a resistance to this natural flow. The threat of annihilation, of non-existence is the impetus and drive that fuels all enquiry and desire.

As well as seeking to grasp and to change (for the better) the time-mind will just as vigorously attempt to prevent natural change, preferring the status quo of stability and safety. This is merely a reflection of the ignorance of the time-mind to the truly eternal nature of being which is established in all places and all times beyond form and function, and upon which there is no dependence.

The time-mind seeks validation of itself only because of its inherent faulty perception rooted in self-doubt. Remove this self-doubt and there is no requisite for validation, but neither then is there a mind to make such an evaluation.

Playground Polarities

The lord of unlimited power
Dwells in the heart of all beings,
And by his magic power of illusion,
Causes them to move about like wooden dolls
Fixed on a machine.

Bhagavad Gita

The polarities that are given birth within this dualistic mind are rather like a Childs playground seesaw. The mind is in a state of continual movement chasing from one end of the seesaw to the other in an attempt to remain only within the positive pole, or at the highest point of our analogy. Yet each time it reaches the opposite pole it finds the opposing end rising ever-higher before it. And so the frantic scrambling back and forth ensues. This continues in varying degrees in accordance with the strength of identification with the character. All dualistic concepts stand at each end of this seesaw; good - bad, rich -

poor, comfort - discomfort, anger - peace, love - hate etc. There is actually total balance in reality, but appearances or phenomena would seem to state otherwise.

Using this analogy, there is a still point, a point from which all movements can be seen without agitation. This still point is in perfect balance – that is its very nature, yet in and of itself it gives rise to *all possible* movement. In fact without this still point, this fulcrum at the centre of existence, there could be no movement at all. It is of course, right at the heart of all possible movement. It is the nothingness, the emptiness from which all appearance originates. Within this stillness there is no requirement and no desire, there is the source and entirety of being, immediate and present. Pure potentiality. This is the font of all movement, all being, all animation. In this place of non-existence is all existence birthed. Here, at this point, *is all there is. It is everywhere and nowhere, here and now.*

The time-mind arises in agitation, movement is its very nature. Thoughts arise and flow in many directions each giving birth to off-shoots or tributaries of still further mental meanderings. These impulses may be chased with great passion and followed with much sincerity, as the perpetual swing in polarities continues. Eventually they will be observed and the frenetic swing will dissipate until the still point is once again discovered, where all movement coalesces into simple presence of being.

Movement is the nature of phenomenal being, the agitation from one polarity to the other, created by thought, by contemplation. This vibration is the ignition of appearance in time and space. Thought – mind stuff, is what the time-mind regards as objective reality – *there is no objective reality, for there is no subject separate from any object.* In our analogy of the seesaw or counterbalance, the source of every movement is nothing! Complete stillness beyond movement and form – and so it is at the very heart of appearance is…..emptiness.

The Tree

*Nowhere does there exist the one who
Is the cause of mental activity.
And yet, since activity exists, how can
you say that such activity does not arise?
Since merely allowing thoughts to settle
into their own condition, without trying
to modify them in any way, is sufficient,
How can you say that you are not able to
remain in a calm state?*

(Padmasambhava)

All errors arise from this one simple but fundamental error; that there is a separate individual with a separate personality, with volitional choice of thought and action.

Reading this statement from an individuals egoic perspective would seem to make a total nonsense. But lets be really clear here in what is being said.

There is only the *appearance* of individuality.

The appearance is a result of false *interpretation*.

Interpretation is a direct result of *a mental state*.

The mental state is an *illusion* - there is only *beingness* which is wholly undivided and in which all appearance arises *spontaneously*.

Therefore individuality is merely a false notion in time.

Again we must return to the analogous approach to give a clearer indication as to where this narrative is pointing. Take the example of a tree. Let us say our tree represents the entire sphere of both subtle and gross phenomenal activity; all universes; all realms and all galaxies; all notions of space and all time that ever was or could ever be. In fact our tree represents every notional thought in every notional mind that ever notionally existed, containing all and every aspect of life, each and every possibility. (Quite a specimen you would have to agree!)

Just so that we are really clear on this point – Let us restate that there is absolutely nothing that exists outside or separate from our analogical tree.

The nature of the tree is pure and whole, demonstrating this wholeness of nature by expanding and branching out more and more of itself in an out flowing of eternal impulse and infinite idea, imbuing

The Tree

all its branches of impulse with the self same creative nature it possesses. It is literally giving birth to ever more of itself in thought-form, simply by the process of self-contemplation. Forming myriad expressions in bewildering array and diversity as it's branches sprout forth and likewise create yet further branches. There is no limit to its growth, it is a limitless tree, it encompasses all – it *IS* all. And yet, strangely, it occupies no space whatsoever, nor is it reliant upon time for its growth. All it ever conceived is here, right now.

The time-mind - this seeming individuality – is represented in this analogy by a branch of this tree. But a branch believing (absurdly) in it's *isolation* from the tree itself, who perceives growth in linear terms, but who's very being, who's very existence is undeniably tree-ness!

It is bizarre indeed to suppose a branch could exist without its source - the tree. And since all there is *is* tree, it's true nature must be also tree-ness, Containing and imbued with all characteristics of tree-ness.

It does not have to become anything, to change or to improve or attain any other quality because the fact is that it can never become anything less that it's complete tree-ness already existing.

There is simply no place where tree-ness ends and Branch-ness begins. No, it is one whole and complete unicity of Tree-ness.

Likewise in our functioning. The personality believes in its isolation as branch-ness, waving wildly in the treetop it looks across to other branches likewise blowing about in this analogical breeze, and it sees only from this perspective of separation. This mistaken identity is however only brought about through an error of perception. The appearance of an individual with it's body-mind suggests separation or isolation in branch-ness. But this false association arises out of the denial it's source; out of the claiming of separateness, of characteristics in isolation to the eternal being (Tree) giving life to it all. Rather than looking across (outwardly) at the external appearances it has only to take a different perspective, to observe the true nature of it's existence, downward (inward observation)) in our analogy to our root and branch nature, and sure enough we behold our undivided tree-ness. Seeking within that which was never absent. And so *"What God has joined no man can put asunder"* purely because it would be impossible to do so!

This attempted divorce of being, this denial, is the only difference between the awakened and unawakened state of consciousness. In Truth the separated state simply does not exist, being impossible. Life is whole and complete. Yet the delusional time-mind in its insistence in this division will make it seem possible, but again only through the error of perspective. It is this and only this dreaming state that gives rise to all suffering and discomfort, to all unfulfilled striving and desire, to all seeking.

Such is the nature of mind or consciousness that it believes itself to be what it *sees itself to be*. Such is the loving directive of the Tree; to allow consciousness (all its branches) to be that which it desires to be. If consciousness believes itself to be a tree, then tree-ness will be its experience, whole and undivided, if branch-ness, then branch-ness will be the experience – though NOT the reality. The Tree remains the one and only tree existing in the immediacy of now.

Consciousness dances upon the ocean of context and form, upon a backdrop of space and time.

It is a cosmic game of oceanic proportions - a hide and seek scenario - in which the both hunter and hunted interplay, discovering and remaining hidden all at once!

For within the reality of the tree there is 'nowhere' separate from anywhere else, it all resides here and it all takes place now. There is nowhere to get to and nothing to gain.

The life story can be a wonderful experience, a marvellous departure. To touch, smell, taste, see and hear - to fall in Love, to lose, to grieve, to cry and to dance in euphoria. A sensual, glorious play of multi-faceted existence, life for life's sake, without meaning or necessity.

The enjoyment can recede however , when our old adversary ''meaning' is sought. When the 'why's' appear, when reason is desired. When the freedom and carefree abandon that accompanies present enjoyment, is dissolved in the angst ridden battle to remain polarised, opinionated and intentionally focussed.

When the seesaw of life is not ridden and enjoyed for the sheer pleasure, but the frantic and exhausting attempt to remain at the highest point is pursued with all too fleeting success and ultimate disappointment, the inherent enjoyment is overlooked in the chasing.

Yet all that is required is vision. Clarity to see what is always present and what has never been absent. *I am nothing without the father*. My existence, this existence, this very life is rooted in present being and ever will be my home and my source.

Whilst I seek to be right, to stand proud and superior the external multitude, I remain locked in a hierarchy of duality, a duality constructed in time by a mind in turmoil and agitation, an imprisonment of meaninglessness.

The Pool

Space is the geometry of time

Terry Edwards

The crystal pool of present being lies completely motionless, a clarity that is undisturbed and absolutely without agitation, direction or desire. It's very nature is clear and unified within itself, requiring nothing to embellish or enhance it's inherent perfection, unaffected and undifferentiated by concepts of space or time.

The time-mind is the agitation which ripples the surface, that creates the dance of drama. A disturbance that the pool appears to adopt with the introduction of the notion of space-time. Now reaching, grasping and seeking seems possible within a tension filled amnesia, forming the waves of motion in materialisation. But let it not be forgotten that this disturbance is pure mental apparition. The reality of the crystal pool remains constant despite the *apparency of agitation.* It is only with the observation of the motion, in seeing that pure being is ever-present, that agitation or disturbance can abate and a recognition of the true nature of the pool be apprehended. This is not brought about by any volitional action of a fictitious doer, but is rather, simply seen – the pool in clarity giving rise to all possible agitation.

The time-mind is the idea agitation alone. Without the notion of time there is no possibility of anticipation, evaluation, contemplation or projection. All these attributes are fundamental to the existence and projection of time and clearly only a creation of a superimposed idea of present insufficiency. Somewhere, somehow there is a concept that present being is lacking, and it is within this very singular but disruptive idea that all forms of deficiency are born. The mirage created from this singular error is viewed at the expense of the loss of tranquillity in the eternal present stillness of the pool of eternal being.

The racing and chasing of the mind is never fulfilled, this perpetual motion can be a camouflage to the crystal stillness which sources all. The time-mind is the impostor that alone would claim sovereignty to peace and happiness, but which would only ever seek it in time - tomorrows peace, next weeks happiness, next years fulfilment. The deception of the time-mind will overlook the natural peace that resides simply as a permanent function of present being. This one tiny denial is all that gives life to the idea of some future hope or promise, always just a step or two out of present reach will the time-mind hold its illusive promise, and in doing so stir the waters in the pool of eternal being.

The Pool

But where is this one who disturbs the water? Can the water be separate from it's apparent agitation, if all there is *is* the crystal pool of being, who is it that would disturb the tranquillity - How could this be possible?

Clearly *it is not possible*, it is not so, it is nothing other than a mere fiction - a story. The dream of the time-mind plying its song of separation, confusion and pretence upon a back drop deficiency and deprivation, a story wholly without foundation and a story ultimately bound to crumble in the crystal light of present being.

The pool of being lies undisturbed and unperturbed, nonchalant to the rantings and ravings of the frenetic thought processes and passionate desires of the personality locked in time. The pool of present being lies secure and safe, untouched by the fickle hand of time, impenetrable to strange notions and deluded fantasies of paucity and lack, ever open to it's rediscovery beyond the dream landscape of imagination and anarchy.

Goal Orientation

Change comes about without intention

Eric Baret

To set a goal of any kind is to place one's attention away from the now. It is a future desire, a promise of peace, and it is a prison. All processes and paths are products of mind that hold out an illusory promise of future liberation whilst keeping the reality of present liberation hidden from view. It is avoidance of the obvious and it is wholly fictitious.

What seems so incredibly difficult from a personal perspective is the idea that there is nothing to seek; that what is sought is wholly and immediately present in the beingness, the awareness of this very moment. But due to this bizarre orientation, this isolated idea of self-in-time seeks to satiate it's self-created longing in those places and in those material objects and situations in which lasting peace or fulfilment can never be found.

Let it be stated clearly once again that *the future is a total fabrication it does not exist*. There is only this moment, right now. The avoidance of now, is the avoidance of seeing with clarity, with truth. It is insanity to seek outside of now, yet this is what the egoic mind endeavours to perpetuate. The projected guilt of previous actions is yet another device used to maintain the idea of identity and temporal reality, another trick to avoid the present availability of being..

To truly see the mind story *as a story* is real freedom - the recognition of the immediacy of a freedom that always exists. Why? Because there is no longing for future fulfilment. The desire for things to be different than they are right now, be it emotionally, physically or mentally, is the only cause of suffering. The notion that my peace and joy lie on the horizon will keep them right there – out of 'my' reach, and place 'me' in the firm grip of the fantasy of unfulfilled desire.

This persistent yearning to change the way things are or were, arises because of this false identification with the time-mind, simply because this deceptive promise is accepted as achievable and attainable.

There is however, the opportunity *right now* to *not want* anything; the opportunity *right now* to just allow this present moment to be as it is. If we seek anything (as contradictory as this may sound) it is to seek to observe this process of wanting change; to simply notice the desiring mind telling its story, and in that seeing, noticing how life is unfolding effortlessly and quite naturally within the totality of this awareness. This can be discovered through observation of the process of mind.

The apparent difficulty is always is seeing things for what they are – mere appearances. The time-mind in its hypnotic dance of attainment, locks the focus externally in it's attempt at justifying a phantom Individual existence. Yet in simply experiencing feelings free from attachment as the arising of form and sensation and nothing more, despite the temptation to label them pleasant or uncomfortable, then it can begin to be seen that there is no need for alteration, no matter what is happening; anger, depression, loneliness, exhilaration, excitement, hatred, disappointment. All of it is the arising of life in its myriad forms and it has no impact whatsoever upon the wholly unblemished unconditioned awareness which is aback and giving rise to the entirety - this is the True nature of being.

'Wanting what you have' then, can never be a successful directive as such, for there is no real ownership in any sense, though it is a popular instruction in the current self-help climate. Yet if it were a simple case of accepting 'my' neurosis, 'my' anger, 'my' lack of compassion, 'my' fear of failure and so on *ad infinitum*, then you can bet that 'I' am just as equally accepting 'my' story as a reality and all that goes with that erroneous stance. In doing this I am merely rearranging the circumstances of the projection to another aspect of the story. And then we are back into the realm of psychoanalysis and further mental elaboration, further story telling.

Wanting what you have is not an instruction that the time-mind would ever accept. Why? Because it is the one invitation, the one immediate concept (right now) that this personality centred perspective cannot survive. To suggest the personality can wholly accept this moment is a nonsense. The personality is, by nature, a character of time, of resistance, of avoidance.

It may appear to accept certain aspects of life, but generally it is not acceptance at all, but a simple question of replacement, adopting another focus, another avenue of thought, another distraction, an arising of perpetual hope.

It is only in present awareness, when the mental dialogue has ceased that freedom is present – for no one! These are the times spoken of earlier, creative times when we comment 'I was lost in the moment,' (but notice the personality has returned to evaluate and claim its part in the experience).

Once again we are drawn to simple observation of what is, and within that observation discovering perhaps the Truth behind the appearance.

If we observe the 'natural' world we can see quite clearly. The absence of angst and the presence of natural grace in action.. The most natural and functional way of being possible.

The creative Mind functions likewise, in the instant. Works of great beauty, pleasure and impact are not thought–out methodically as such, with reference to a previous model, but arise within the natural spontaneity life in the moment.

Goal Orientation

Of course there seems to be a functional aspect to mind, that works in an apparent logical fashion, constructing buildings, communicating instructions, cooking foods for sustenance, rearing children and tending land for example. But such is the multifaceted nature of mind in time. The story of 'me' in time is an elaborate and complex drama, the scope of set and stage are magnificent in design and form. The life story is grand indeed. But in and of itself it has no meaning, *yet this is it's true glory*. It is not going anywhere, there is nothing to achieve outside of it's own expression – it is life everlasting, and who could truly say that the appearance of life need be anything outside of *this*?

A Life of Avoidance

You wander from room to room
Hunting for the diamond necklace
That is already around your neck!

Rumi

So the everyday perspective of individuality in time is a continual self-deception, an attempt to climb to the heights of the seesaw ever rising before us. Spending lives chasing and grasping, ever in anticipation or expectation, from what was, to what could or might be, in avoidance of what is, right now. Like the proverbial fish swimming around in the ocean in search of water.

It may be equated to the needle on an old vinyl record player. The sound of the record is only ever produced at the very point of contact. The only active and truly functioning aspect of the equipment is right at that very point of contact.

So too with this thing called life. Everything is happening right now, right here at the *tip of the needle experience* ! This is our only point of contact – the now. Feel it, smell it, touch it, taste it – there is nothing else! Being is here, now. Nowhere, no place or time exists other than this. This very moment is, and contains all of your tip of the needle experience!

All other considerations that arise such as memory or anticipation, they too happen here and now at the tip of our needle of awareness, but they are illusions within the storytellers realm that would project a belief in a future sound somewhere other than where the needle rests, but no tune could ever exist there, there is no possibility of sound without a needle to procure it.

Beingness is the needle – the immediate, only ever right here. Timeless being arises spontaneously at the very pinnacle of life right now, it is so absolutely immediate, how could it possibly ever be avoided? How crazy would it be to suggest there is somewhere other that this place of contact with being – there simply is *no other place, no other time. Life is here now, what you are and always will be.*

This projected life story is an avoidance of present awareness, the repetition from past to future forming an arc of deception, of continuity over what is right here.. If I am locked into the time-mind perspective, I am locked also into this concept of continuity, of avoidance of the here and now.

But again, this is the nature of the time-mind perspective, part and parcel of the clothing adopted for the drama. These words may be a reminder that it is possible to be *aware* of the story. There is simply an idea that some minds exist in sheer blissful ignorance as they immerse themselves completely and wholly into character play, this is another concept of story-telling and is, of course, absolutely fine. An avoidance of the present moment is just that - a way of being or living, and though it may seem to be limiting, it remains simply an experience.

What should be done then. How should 'I' live in order to accomplish this feat of awareness to free 'myself' of strife? It does not matter at all what is done. The doing is quite irrelevant. The mighty lion or colossal whale are not pondering their own existence but living it. The flea and the frog are not fraught with tension, but natural life arising. Intellect, self-awareness is life being self-aware – there is no object. Being is its own reason for living, for this is what is always occurring.

There can simply be no directive, to do so would suggest that action can lead to the pure awareness that is already present. Let the action be what it will be. Let the impetus to move in a certain direction be just that – and follow it or do not. It is not within the action that freedom from the dictatorial time-mind exists, but in the *seeing of the attachment to it' story telling*, and within that seeing, within the observation, comes freedom from dogmatic addiction.

Content and Confusion

A billion times God has turned man into himself

Hafiz

When we live life from an individual perspective, what we do seems to hold great import. Opinion, belief, identity, ambition and drive are considered very positive attributes for much of the world story. Ideas of gaining and improving in time are likewise established as guiding principle of an objective world view..

What is often overlooked however, is that once these goals are achieved, once the aims are met, another goal lies waiting to be achieved. This perpetual striving is fine of itself, but when seen as the route *to something* – this is where the error of time-mindedness creeps in. Sure enough there can be momentary satisfaction, but the goal identified time-mind will generate that persistent little question upon which rests its very life-blood – 'What now?' And once more the ever-distant horizon appears to hold promise.

All aspects of life are just that – aspects of life. The moment I enter the 'right/wrong' debate I am back into relative territory, the bi-polar swing of opposites.

The analogy of life as a dance rather than a journey is a sound one. There is something very striking and immediate about this concept that instantly illuminates and allows a freedom to see all previously cherished concepts as simply the fabric of the dance.

The *content* of life is where the focus of attention lies when it is believed that 'our' own stories are the only reality, when we know ourselves only as the character of the play we are locked into this self-improvement cycle and strive to change and to better within a hierarchical state of mind, to protect and to safeguard our vulnerable existence. Self-improvement may take the form of a 'better' job, a larger salary, an enhanced recognition with greater status, it may even take the seemingly opposite direction, a down-sizing to achieve greater peace, less stress, less responsibility etc or a myriad of other likely candidates. However the root of all these desires, irrespective of the form, lies in a fundamental sense of present incompletion or lack that inevitably arises within the idea of a separated time-mind.

Deep down it knows it's falseness, it's wholly fictitious nature and this is what gives rise to the perpetual search for completion, but this is directed externally to outward conditions. But as Jean Klein once commented..

Content and Confusion

"What you are is without direction".

The moment a finite direction is sought a limitation is put in place upon that which is limitless, and as consciousness experiences itself as what it believes itself to be, the story of insufficiency is perpetuated.

Content, what goes on within the story, is simply an aspect of the dance. It matters not in which direction one dances which steps one takes, for *the joy of the dance is in the dancing* itself, not in arriving at any destination.

When life is seen as a journey then there is a desire to reach that goal, a need to take a certain route, to travel at certain speed. All these criteria are fabrications superimposed upon life, all of which serve to limit and detract from the *present* experience. There is an ever-present voice of reason giving instructions, checking operations, implementing safety measures, assessing risk and so forth.

Of course direction and desire are fine in and of themselves, but they are merely constituents of the content of life, and when seen as such they can be enjoyed as the arising of form and function within life's dance.

The snag is, they are rarely seen within this context, but rather are held as the fundamental guiding principles of life. When this is so, rules and restrictions are placed upon society, moral and ethical codes of conduct are instigated and adopted as norms of behaviour. These blinkers we place upon our eyes give us a rather jaundiced view. Now we are once more plunged into the rights and wrong of life, the polarities of good and evil and into the realms of justice in which all seeds of conflict lie.

There is no limit to the influence of this polarised and distorted perspective, it colours it's world with pungently flavoured beliefs, creating Gods of wrath and destruction that would threaten all who would stand opposed to the 'good' it represents. It is rooted in division and conflict, constructing behavioural rules and regulations that are given a 'holy' irreproachable authority.

There is no denying however, they are staggeringly good yarns, rich with hierarchy and heroism, full of contrast and colour, to be enjoyed and played to the full. It is only when the drama is taken seriously and one becomes lost in the myth and mayhem that suffering is born.

But again let us remember, this too is the dance. There is nothing that is not the dance! The secret is to recognise the dance - to observe. To watch what is arising without attachment to the outcome, to abandon compulsion in favour of freedom. *To be in the world but not of it.*

So be daring. look at your beliefs. Even better, look to see who's beliefs they truly are and who it is that would look at them at all! From where did they come and to whom do they apply? Notice how they shift and alter in time and location, notice too how they are dropped and adopted for different circumstances and company. And notice finally, perhaps, that all this change is mere fabrication, wholly unreal and ultimately meaningless. Embrace the dance for the sake of dancing freely.

The Imagination of Psychology

The dissection of the false will never reveal Truth.

Anon

Life stories, as has been repeated frequently now, are products of the time-mind. It is a ingenious if somewhat flawed condition. In order to maintain this reality as a whole and functioning entity of existence, the time-mind creates a web of complexity within which it would seek to establish its existence. Paradoxically, even these words, this very sentence, if claimed by an individual would be that self same pretence - the superimposed personality - claiming the production of this volume, but which, in actuality, is simply the arising naturally of spontaneous action.

Psychology is a fascinating world indeed. But it too is nothing other than the product of story-teller mind seeking to further establish its reality. It does this of course by further division and dissection. These mental gymnastics are deceptions which further subdivide the story (of the mind's own functioning) into yet smaller classifications. It spins historical yarns of its influences and nature to give the story greater credulity and realism. It remains wholly fiction. Rooted in belief in an objective world, with body and mind as a separate volitional individuality (the doer or chooser).

Now again, this forms the fabric of the life story that is being adopted with humanity as a whole as the backdrop, just as equally as say evolution or biology form their own narrative within the structure of this apparent existential story. It is a scenario of stories within stories, as all relative scenario's are. Constructs of the time-mind in the play of life. Constructs which seem to tie together innumerable aspects of the story, but which ultimately only ever arise presently.

The problem (relatively speaking) with psychological approaches to life (from the perspective of the one who would seek lasting peace) is that the very peace which is sought within the examination of the working of the mind, are themselves fantasy. The same false assumption exists throughout the whole process of psychological investigation, namely that there is an individual, and within that initial error that something is 'wrong' with that individual, perhaps something missing, something lacking, something to improve, to change. There simply is not and never could be.

It is a situation where the seeking of freedom or sanctity within the story is attempted by analysing and dissecting a wholly fictitious set of assumptions in order to find meaning – *One cannot find meaning in the meaningless no matter how hard one tries or how long one may look.*

The assumptions may be well studied, researched and the remedies well implemented, indeed overwhelming proof will be offered in support of all claims that the mind can be understood as a functioning entity and this may indeed seem to offer comfort, respite and reasoning for those characters involved. But we are once again unavoidably enmeshed in the matter of temporality, both recollection and projection of stories that are offered as an intellectual means to effect change.

The organism comprising body and mind are clearly linked within this existential play of life, but dissection and analysis of this illusional character reveals only further fantasy. It equates nicely to a hologram that can be divided in a million different ways only to reveal identical content and substance throughout.

Psychology is based upon the assumption that there are functional and dysfunctional forms of behaviour, positive and negative attributes. It is a relative discipline in a relative context. It is yet another story - An imagination of mind. For if we examine only briefly what me mean by dysfunctional behaviour, we will be confronted once again with the obvious; that an action is labelled functional or dysfunctional *only upon the basis of the desired outcome in time* – a relative, not an absolute.

To illustrate; let us use another simple analogy; Say we have a machine designed specifically to produce vanilla ice cream. Now, should that machinery begin producing gooseberry yoghurt, chocolate fudge Sundae, or strawberry cheese cake, we could reasonably agree that, *based upon the desired result,* the machine is dysfunctioning. However, should I be inclined to accept anything that is produced, even though I am aware of the original intention of the machinery, the 'dysfunction' would now be relegated to mere quirk, foible or function. I may still enjoy the product as equally as the intended result, even though it does not comply with the original specifications.

There are of course more 'real' and emotionally charged examples of what we term dysfunction, such as biological dysfunctions; cancer, heart disease, stroke and so forth, which, from the temporal human standpoint can seem devastating, there is no doubt that these forms of 'illness' are highly emotive, producing considerable internal reactions which arise from attachment to preferences. But wouldn't it be fascinating to ponder what the perspective of the cellular microscopic world would be to such 'dysfunction?' to ponder whether the is infinite is 'human minded' at all?

Of course it is where we believe we stand within the context of the story that determines the reaction; Who we think we are, our very core beliefs form the essential fabric of this experience. Remove those barriers and a whole world of difference is revealed.

But now we have introduced another element, not only are we looking at outcome – at goal orientation, for It is not only the desired outcome that effects the ultimate judgement, but the perspective one views *from*, a perspective which is strongly influenced fundamentally by who or what I believe I am (within the story).

But the less a specific outcome is desired; the less investment in the taking of a certain direction, the less disappointed and inclined to judge and label things 'wrong' there is.

This is not a missive set out to disparage passion and drive however. Passion, drive and commitment to a person, cause or destination need not be abandoned in favour of some kind of detached, passive, surrendered state. The action can be what it will – and indeed *will* be what it will.

When a personally identified time-mind discovers that there is no ultimate destination in life, there can be a fine line between seeing life as futile and exhilarating. Futile because the highly charged stories can suddenly seem pointless, yet exhilarating because there is an immense freedom within that very pointlessness.

Imagine if you can, how it would feel to have all that same intensity of feeling and drama within your life story, but with an awareness that ultimately you couldn't get any of it wrong; that nothing was ever lost; that you would never come out of any experience less than you began it – despite what appearances may suggest; That no matter what the temporary result, everything would always be okay because of this eternal cosmic safety net called existence. How would that life story feel now? How much more freely is the trapeze artist able to glide effortlessly through the air knowing his safety net lays strong and secure beneath him? How much more daring his aerial tricky now? Should he fall – *So what?*

If there is no awareness of this safety net, then the reality and trepidation of the action can be acute. This is where we have to introduce our own external safety measures, this is where we have to implement restrictions and safeguards to secure our piece of life from the grip of impending attack or disaster. For if one feels intrinsically vulnerable or fragile, life will be conducted accordingly. Yet even within ancient scriptural stories we are given glimpses of the eternal truths…

> *"Yeah though I walk through the valley of the shadow of death I shall fear no evil, for thou art with me"*
>
> *23rd Psalm*

This familiar passage is often interpreted in the traditional sense, as their being a benevolent creator - a separate entity – a protector waiting in the wings of existence. Yet the present reality is *that this is the nature of being right now*. Life - it's own immediate benevolence.

Relative existence, seeming to be an experience of contrast, is an experience rooted in choice, one thing over another, in which life is generally regarded as the 'journey' spoken of earlier, with beginning, content and end. Rather than the dance which possess neither beginning or end, but consists only of present content. The linear perspective sees a defined route and an ultimate destination. The circular perspective has no such definition. Neither is there any particular destination, the circular perspective can only accurately be seen as the ever present movement of life, imbued with present enjoyment. The open palm as opposed to the clenched fist. Life arises from the benevolence of being itself without condition.

My Precious Opinion

If man knew himself he would not be mislead by opinions.
Man is made of opinion and his life is a warfare
like all other lives before him.

Phineas P. Quimby

What would life be like without my opinions? How could I possibly ever make my mark; stand up for my rights, fight my corner or express my point of view? Surely my opinions are part of me! How would I ever get my fair share, put right all the injustices, champion my cultural heritage and fight for the freedoms of this world? How could I simply express who I am without my all important authority of opinion?

Well, here's another very short exercise: I am going to suggest something to you and I would like you to assess on a scale of say 1 to 5 just how much of a resistance you have to this suggestion. (5 being the most resistant, 1 being near or complete agreement) okay? Here goes....

> *...Your opinions are worthless and count for absolutely nothing!*

What did you score? I would suggest higher you score the more precious and real your sense of self is to you. (But that's only my opinion!)

Opinions are 'my' claim to know how thing really are. Opinions are the rules and guides by which I regulate my position in life, they are the fruits of my struggle. They reinforce my history and sense of individuality; my persona, they are an intrinsic part of my being, making me who I believe I am, aren't they?.

Well no, actually what opinions really are, are facets of the character driven time-mind, in truth they are the same old delusional ideas we have been discussing throughout these pages. Let it be stated once again that there is nothing wrong with delusional ideas, they simply exist as a functioning and nature of temporal existence. But opinions indicate just how involved is this awareness with this character; by the degree that it experiences resistance or pain when it's opinions are disregarded, thwarted or challenged, by that degree is it invested characterisation – or polarization.

Opinions are defence and attack both. They proclaim the polarised stand real and meaningful, this goal-orientation, this hope for things to turn out the way they 'should,' because 'I' believe 'I' *know* what's best, what's fair for 'me,' and probably what's right and fair for others too! After all 'I' am a reasonable, honest and kind of person.

Yet opinions are the Ideals that lead to my isolation, demons masquerading as angels, inert fabrications in the guise of noble truths, they are my script and direction for the role I play, locking the door to the awareness of my true Self – as unlimited potential. They imprison me in my own desire to be right and condemn me to see with only temporal vision.

A story is neither right nor wrong, it has no ultimate goal and no meaning other than that which the story teller places upon it. It is not a finite or singular event, but a rich and limitless field of experience. A wonderment of expression in itself. But the moment there is a seeking to grasp and become rigid in view the more the narrowing of the horizon begins as 'my' story takes hold.

When there is simply the observing of these opinions, it may be noticed that within that very observation, within that gap created between observer and observed, lies a key to the liberation from identification with that story, longer being held captive to false ideas of authority and it's inherent limitations. Now the potency and addictiveness of destinations lose their grip. The guard can be dropped and insistence dissolved by simple preference.

Observation is the revealer of the narrator and narrative both, affording simple and immediate recognition of the story *as a story*.

Now it may be that some characters simply enjoy being blindly immersed in the drama and seek no other way of being, it would *appear* that this is the case for many. But after any length of time interest can shift or a natural maturing occur, and a seeking for a different experience can arise. This puts me in mind of another familiar text…

"When I was a child, I spoke like a child, I thought like a child, I reasoned like a child. When I became a man, I put childish ways behind me. Now we see but a poor reflection as in a mirror; then we shall see face to face. Now I know in part: then I shall know fully, even as I am fully known.

(Corinthians 1:13)

Opinions are playthings, nothing more than elements of the story, childish characterisational quirks; conditionings or flavours. Yet the more they are held dearly like precious jewels of protection, the taller they build the fortresses that shields true sight – the truly liberating vision.

Truth is. From a temporal perspective, we actually never truly know what anything means. It is only ever relative to where we stand; to who we think we are; to this conditioned mind and everything a limited view entails.

My Precious Opinion

An ancient Zen story illustrates this wonderfully, it is the story of a farmer and his son:

One day the farmer's prize stallion escapes the corral. It was the farmers only form of wealth, his most valuable asset.

The villagers hearing of this 'misfortune' all exclaimed their sorrow to the farmer at this most 'unfortunate event.' "what terrible luck" they cried.

But the farmer was a wise man and simply replied " maybe."

A few days later however, the stallion returned and trailing in its wake were another 10 stallions of equal stature and worth.

The villagers, hearing of this news, all ran to exclaim their joy at the good fortune of the Farmer .." What wonderful good fortune has come your way!" they cried.

But the farmer was a wise man and simply replied… " maybe"

The following week whilst breaking-in one of the wild stallions the farmer's son who, being the only fit able bodied person in the family, taking care of all the chores on the farm, was violently thrown from the horse breaking his leg in two places.

The villagers hearing of this 'misfortune' all ran to exclaim their sorrow to the farmer at this most unfortunate event.' "what terrible luck!" they cried.

But the farmer was a wise man and simply replied… "maybe"

A few days later the National Army was conscripting men for active duty on the front line, a duty that meant almost certain death.

Seeking out and conscripting only the fit and able young men of the village.

Of course, the farmers son was not eligible for duty due to his state of incapacity and was consequently not conscripted.

The villagers, hearing of this news, all ran to exclaim their joy at the good fortune of the farmer .." what wonderful good fortune has come your way!" they cried.

But the farmer was a wise man and simply replied… "maybe"

…And so the story continues without ever reaching a conclusion or destination.

Of course the point being that time-mind never actually knows what an event means at any isolated moment, nor it's implications, but it projects the drama of it's insistence that it does. How powerfully enriching and freeing to be able to break the shackles of this arrogance by proclaiming with great certainty – "I know absolutely nothing" More aptly perhaps – there is nothing to know!

Yet there are grand and elaborate societal structures which seek to proclaim quite the opposite; to reinforce this arrogant assumption of universal wisdom, it is called the 'The law of the land.' We have rooms filled floor to ceiling with volumes of learned texts to back up this 'knowledge' of relative wisdom, proclaiming that it is a categorically certainty what is right, good and proper in the context of a 'civilized society'. Justice systems are fabrications of mind based upon particular perspectives, using temporal experience as an aid to future function. Yet intellect has no capacity to judge. Reasoning is not

My Precious Opinion

Justice, reasoning is intellectual evaluation based on opinion within a temporal setting, taken from a particular perspective.

The most profound truth is that 'I simply do not know anything'. In that Admission there is the opportunity to be open to all possibilities and free from self-limitation. But the character, the story-telling mind, is insistent, and within this insistence lies the chain of all limitation and suffering.

Opinions give birth to war, to famine, to hatred to all forms of isolation and division. Opinions are the potent elixir of the dreamweaver. The drug of passion and polarisation, the judge and jury of my own imprisonment. Yet once again, in Truth they are nothing but apparitions of desire, meaningless and without power lest that power be granted by surrogate belief.

Now

If I didn't remember the past and was unable to speculate about the future, all that would be happening would exist only now.

Anton Vetroff

There is a very subtle difference between having a desire in the way things turn out, and being a detached observer. In the former there is a clinging and needing for events to work out in a particular or 'favourable' fashion – this is investment. This polarisation is not 'wrong' in any sense, it is simply a way of being.

Detached observation encompasses all, uniting polarities, including the invested character. We don't have to curb any action or thoughts, it is not a question of change as has been repeated many times now. If there is great involvement in the storytelling then so be it! It can be observed or otherwise, and who can say which that will be?

Beyond Belief

This is not a prescription for enlightenment, there is no such road map, despite what stories of world religions would proclaim. Only a journey requires a map of instruction, a dance can be free and without boundary or restriction.

Observation is such a simple and ordinary immediacy. It is a question of noticing the present moment absent of the accompanying dialogue, seeing that the one who lives *is* life itself, without separation between subject and object; existence doing what it does in this moment – existing!

Life is eternal. Eternity is now. We play a game of temporary existence in a temporary world of appearances – of comings and goings, and yet all we ever experience is here, now, this. All else is make-believe. But oh how real yesterday can seem to be, and how worryingly real tomorrow looms. But it is only the belief in this character, its history and future ambition that seems to pull a 'me' out of this present moment, that keeps the movie of 'my' life running in its familiarly linear fashion.

It may be argued that yesterday was real, that 'you' celebrated your Birthday, Anniversary or simply took a stroll in the park. Furthermore you may offer me filmed evidence of this, or show me footage of an event a year ago, ten years or maybe even 100 years ago! You may even sight historical events, display wondrous facts and figures from around the globe of great and even magnificent events. The whole panorama of gruesome and ghastly human history, you may sight all this in support of the reality of this temporal linear existence. And

Now

whilst it is undeniable and cannot be refuted as the *appearance* of life in all its intriguing complexity, there remains only a single sustaining reality; *It is all a product of present awareness*. All else is mere mental manufacture. Only *right now* do I listen to your story of yesterday's calamity, only *right now* do I view a picture of last years celebration, only *right now* do I dream of tomorrows glory, only *right now* read historical stories and *only now* do I ever exist at all.

Investment in the time-story does not advance beyond the belief in temporality. It dwells in the hope of things to come, in anticipation and reflection as true and meaningful. It remains blind to its eternal limitless nature.

The full enjoyment and complete involvement of the life story can never truly be taken from a relative, limited standpoint. Only once life is seen in its eternality, in its delightful expression for expressions sake, can it be truly seen through the eyes of that innocent child of being. To have past guilt, anguish and future fear dissolve into the sheer exhilaration of the only true and present moment there ever is - the now, is to take that immortal leap from temporality to presence, from a perpetually potential hell to an ever-present Heaven, from the distant horizon and back home to the land beyond fearful dreams – beyond belief itself and into eternal being.

Love

*Every word of every tongue
Is love telling a story to her own ears
Every Thought in every mind,
She whispers a secret to her own Self.*

*Every Vision in every eye,
She shows her beauty to her own sight.
Every smile on every face,
She reveals her own joy for herself to enjoy.*

*Love courses through everything,
No, Love IS everything.
How can you say, there is no love,
When nothing but love exists?*

*All that you see has appeared because of love.
All shines from Love,
All pulses from Love,
All flows from Love -
No, Once again , all is Love.*

(Fakhruddin Araqi)

All the intellectual wisdom in the world is indeed as a resounding cymbal, a hollow and echoing chasm, without a depth of connection to a certain indefinable pureness, a strange and ineffable quality which lies at the heart of all existence, which ignites the very spark of all life, thought and action, and what that is, we only know as 'Love.'

There is something at the heart of all creation, something which cannot be known and yet remains closer than each and every breath we draw. Nearer and infinitely more 'real' than the myriad images that flicker and dance across these eager senses. More enchanting and beguiling than any story I may lustfully engage with. It is the source and substance of all life in all its forms and functions, it imbues and pervades all notions of space and time, remaining elusively ever-present, confounding and yet comforting, the hidden orchestrator of all – being itself.

We have used the term 'God,' 'Allah,' 'Jehovah,' 'The Father' and many many other symbolic references to attempt capture this wondrous liberation, this supreme creative principle, imposing morality, personality and preference upon this entirely inexplicable source of being.

Yet it could as easily be referred to as' Infinite Love,' for this wholly ineffable force, this mighty impulse embraces every possible materialisation of thought form, every concept ever given birth in mind, and every single identity ever adopted in apparent space-time. Though this is not a love of selection or discrimination, for those attributes are only to be found in the arena of the limited humanistic perspective; a love that seeks reciprocation, reward or fulfilment of certain criteria; a love that is restricted or reserved for the worthy, righteous or favoured. This is not Love unconditional, but a highly conditioned behaviour arising from the conditioned mind.

No, Eternal, Infinite Love is a Love that is completely free of condition, It is the unconditioned nature itself, without form, or destination. It is Love that has no prerequisites or qualifications for acceptance. A love that is limitless, ever-present and unrestricted. Giving of itself in all and every situation. The alpha and omega, that imbues life and propels all life stories, characters and concepts. It is creative impulse, it *is* creation itself. It is the very heart and source of all life and is All that there is beyond and giving life to all appearance, it is Life everlasting - Love everlasting - life for life's sake. Absent of meaning or purpose yet containing all meaning and all purpose, for it is the all. It neither questions nor confounds but exists in all places in all time, immediate and impregnable, Observing it's own dance, it is the very *observation* of life itself.

These words are, of course, futile manipulations of ideas which wholly fail to grasp what they seek to describe, falling into meaningless abstraction simply because there is no possible way to approach the unapproachable, the source of all. The closer I advance in intellectual explanation, the further I draw away, such is the paradox of the unspeakable.

'Perhaps you think that different kinds of Love are possible. Perhaps you think there is a kind of love for this, a kind of Love for that; a way of loving one, another way of loving still another. Love is

one. It has no separate parts and no degrees; no kinds nor levels, no divergences and no distinctions. It is like itself, unchanged throughout. It never alters with a person or a circumstance. Love's meaning is obscure to anyone who thinks love can change… It is whole and complete.. a law without opposite'

(A Course in Miracles)

The undivided simplicity of being, the beauty, the freshness of this very moment. The freedom and exhilaration of living life without the repetitive voice of self-condemnation ever passing judgement. The seeing with simple clarity of present awareness. All these things suggest something very immediate, very ordinary, yet all too easily disregarded in favour of the tumultuous rancour of the story telling time-mind.

It would seem that there is an 'I,' an Identity, a character, who lives in a world of opposites, a world of confused dreams, who rides the dualistic roller coaster of trepidation, excitement, pain and pleasure. Who dances the dance of complexity and confusion, occasionally believing he has caught a glimpse of Reality beyond illusions, only to believe the momentary revelation to be a mirage turning to dust before his mortal gaze. A 'someone' who plays hide and seek with his eternal nature, ever-pretending and teasing himself into awakening from his playful slumber. Yet all there is, is Love

Love

I sing the silent song of creation with each flicker of my eyes and each breath from my lips, yet still it passes unnoticed. With each heartbeat that thrusts life through this fleeting vessel, I ride the turbulent waves of relativity, holding fast to the seeming safety and security of familiarity, disguised in form and entranced by feeling. I entrance myself in a captivating display of self-delusion, reborn in each moment from the unfathomable depths of being, my existence given life from this bottomless and inexhaustible sanctity of Love.

In the Stillness of being I remain Forever Here and Now.

Dialogues

Who or what is God?

Firstly, the term 'God' is full of intellectual implication and distortion, it is a concept which has become symbolic of just how the mind attempts to capture that which is beyond it's comprehension. It is a misrepresentation because there is no way for the Infinite to be represented in finite terms. These distortions form the fabric of the historical and religious stories which are given significance only by belief or faith of the mind which indulges *that mythical narrative*. So before any true light can bear upon this question we must know exactly *what it is we are asking* and moreover what is the nature of the questioner itself.

The difficulty with this enquiry arises from the mind that believes itself separate from an objectified world. More simply, a mind that believes in its own isolation. Without this premise of separation there is nowhere and nothing outside of 'this,' and hence infinity/eternity is here now. Simple!

A finite characteristic simply cannot be the nature of the infinite, this is the contradiction. In this sense there is nothing that is not 'God.' Yet this is also misleading, for it can set up the idea that any individual or separate appearance is God in isolation. Yet isolation is not possible, and is not so. The Infinite is complete and cannot be bound nor separated, cannot be finite or particular, it is whole and undivided and that is why it is impossible to speak in limited terms about that which defies containment. Appearance of division in the manifest world is simply the apparent dance of form and function, but the dance is *one dance*.

So what is God? The inexpressible and the unknowable.

But surely there has to be a divine force to ensure fairness and justice otherwise where would we be but in total chaos with no guide or principle to follow?

We need to back up a little here. Firstly, lets us ask who needs this, who or what is it that seeks justice, that seeks fairness and stability? Who exactly is the 'me' you seem to speak of as an entity of will and substance. Take a look at this enquiry first of all and you may discover something quite astonishing. It is possible that you may find that this 'you,' this sense of being at the heart of all these goings on In life, is an aliveness, a sense of being in which the experience of fear, of chaos, of needing security and structure is a concept itself. So an initial observation of the one that seems to demand and dictate can be a most revealing exercise to begin with.

'Divine fairness,' on the other hand, is yet another concept. Judgement and retribution are sought only by that which feels threatened and vulnerable within itself, that which does not know its own nature and as such seeks, in objects or the exterior, that which it feels inherently lacking, this ignorance can take many forms or appearances, being rooted in tension, it gives rise to hatred, anger, resentment, and conflict, all of which demonstrate the intrinsic dissociation from it's own natural nature. This insecurity gives rise to the notion of an externalised almighty entity imbued with the same judgemental characteristics as the human personality possess. The infinite is beyond concept and certainly beyond judgement. Yet all these things can appear *within it*. Appearances take many forms, yet the infinite does not posses finite quality. Clarity itself reveals it's own ultimate and complete sense of balance, but this is not a concept to be understood and acted upon, it is not a relative posture, it is the present, the all in all.

So are you saying it is not God's will that man behave as he does, but that it is man seeing himself separate from God that causes the conflict and upset?

Firstly what is occurring is spontaneous appearance You see once again this question assumes a finite subject-object relationship between *this* 'me' and *that* 'God.' There is an implied limitation or separation between these two apparent aspects. Of course the simple answer is that there *is only God's will*. But you see now we have a contradiction, a paradox. Now the intellect may ask how there can be both ignorance of one's own true nature of being and the totality of God occurring simultaneously. And herein lies the core of all enquiries. Put simply we are led to ask... *'how is it that I can seem to be that which I do not seem to be.'* And once again observation of the one who makes this statement is perhaps the only route to the undoing of the this apparent conundrum. Suffice to say appearances can be most deceptive.

I don't get it, Do you mean I am God or the infinite but don't know it, and if this is the case and I don't know it, how can I not know it, if I am everything there is?

Let's examine this a little further then. Who are you?
David.
What is David
A 48 year old man.
So what you are is a 48 year old body-mind with a label we know as David?

I wouldn't put it that way exactly, I'd say I am much more than that, not just a body-mind.

Such as?

Well, a husband, a loving father, a worker, I have my own quirks and behaviours, I live my own unique life and speak in my own sort of style, there of loads of things that make me who I am.

So are these sets of characteristics *who you are,* and moreover are they constant, in other words, do they never alter, vanish or change over time?

Oh yes, I do change, everybody does, but I am still David.

Yet these characteristics that have changed or been abandoned along the way, give David a different flavour, so to speak, from a previous idea of what David was say 10 years ago?

W*ell, yes but I am still the same man at heart.*

Okay, but your *concept* of yourself has changed. The idea about who you are can therefore, be seen as flexible or inherently changeable in time. So that your idea of who you are alters or shifts; your values, your hopes and aspirations, your outlook, all these conditions change, yet your sense of self at the heart of all this, or perhaps your sense of being, has a quality of stability or constancy beyond definition or description, would that be accurate?

Yes, I suppose, in a way.

This is a good illustration of how one can seem to know and not know one's self, simultaneously as it were. Ideas and concepts of the mind-in-time change, that is the nature of mind – movement, activity, or at least this is the appearance. Yet that which *gives rise to these movements* and activity of thought and impulse, whilst being ever-present and immediate, is beyond change and indeed beyond concept, being eternal and infinite. But it is never *not* present and immediate. The individual changeable self-concept is the delusion, which happens to arise within wholeness – this is the paradox.

You often talk of appearances as being meaningless, this sound awfully sad and makes life seem somewhat pointless.

This is such a common misinterpretation of mind, and here's why; The mind-in-time, who you think you are, with all your life stories, history and conditioning and so forth, seem to make up who you are exclusively, in other words *your idea of who you are* is the only identity you accept. This seems to *mean* something, to have value, to be important, serious one might say. When the term 'meaningless' is used it refers to the reality that *nothing has greater significance than anything else within the appearances of the material world.* In other words, there are no levels, no hierarchies, no better and no worse, no improvements and no advancements –these are labels overlaid onto the material appearance which seems to give it a meaning or coherence *it does not possess independently.* In reality, all there is *is* this infinite dance! The term 'dance' is a powerful metaphor, because generally it is regarded as something to be enjoyed in-the-moment, not because there is an end-goal to strive for.

Now, a dance could just as easily be called meaningless, but it would not makes it any less pleasurable an experience. A glorious sunset could be called meaningless, as indeed it is, absolutely, yet this doesn't necessitate the of viewing it sad encounter.

Walk into any art gallery and view the painting and sculptures on display, there simply is no inherent fixed meaning to those pieces, they can only be engaged with, and within that interaction an experience formed. It is the *apparency* of this subject/object relationship which seems to imbue meaning. Remove this subject object *relationship* and there is absolutely no meaning, absolutely no idea of hierarchy, but an immense and immediate presence, without description or definition, lacking nothing whatsoever, yet giving rise to all.

I have followed spiritual paths that have encouraged denial of desire as the ultimate goal, along with other behavioural restrictions, is this what you mean by observing, watching but not wanting?

Not at all. A spiritual path is a road leading nowhere, as all *paths* do. Try to think in terms of dancing (it's much easier). <u>There is no ultimate goal</u>. This is what seems to be so disappointing to the intellectual time-mind, What is, is here and now. The only real denial is the continual avoidance of this present moment – denying one's own immediacy of being. The mind-in-time seeks for future states of being, reflecting on past states of being, and thus avoiding THIS present beingness! Beingness is not a state.

As to desire it is not 'wrong,' Nothing is 'wrong' with anything. 'Wrong' is purely a concept which supposes there is an incorrect and indeed a correct action that can be taken by a volitional self. Any choice can only *seem* to occur *within time*.

Desire gives rise to anticipation or expectancy, in which there is contained an inherent tension between the apparent present lack or deficiency and it's possible future fulfilment. There is an assumed duality of a 'someone,' an identity, wanting something they do not seem to posses right now. This possession can only be sought in time. The personal identity is entirely a product of this temporal mental concoction. Desire simply perpetuates this illusion. But there is absolutely nothing wrong with it in any sense whatsoever, it is merely appearance.

So what is life?

Expression. This! How else could this question be answered? Life is the immediate awareness that is present right here and right now. It is certainly not quantifiable; there is as much life in an ant as there is in an antelope, as much in a weasel as a whale. Life is the eternal beingness of this moment, which can give rise to an unfathomable diversity of appearances, but only ever in the present awareness that is here and now. What man is apt to incorrectly assume is that life can *only* be animated and that sentience has some kind of privileged status. This hierarchical outlook is a misconception. Survival of the fittest, for example is yet another mental narrative, a story of conflict and struggle, but a wholly imagined one. Life is the background of all appearance. *It is not the appearance* that has life, but rather the ground from which it arises. There is only the unicity of life.

When does life begin and when does it end.

This is the temporal question of the time-mind seeking to further it's seemingly separate material-identified existence with a meaningless enquiry into its own nature. The mind itself is a fabrication. It never began and it never ends. The body is appearance within that fiction.

Life eternal simply is. Being is. Beginnings and endings appear to exist only within a seemingly finite time-mind. All life is continual. In terms of temporal material appearance we could ask does the sperm and egg not already live prior to the conception of a different form by their union? Life does not begin with death. Life begets life – all there is, is life ad infinitum. The fundamental error of interpretation and perception is in seeking meaning within the finite form. *Form has no inherent meaning*, but is merely the vehicle of life in appearance.

What effect does seeing the story of life, as a story, have?

There is no effect for the individual other than the possibility that the story or the drama loses it's ability to entrance the character within it's role. There is no longer an exclusive and automatic role-player, but rather a slightly detached observing element which can defuse the tension caused by an exclusive attachment. Observation is free from the particular perspective and opens up the possibility to clarity. Clarity unflavoured by conditionings of the associations of the temporal mind. There is a common misconception that life will change drastically once the story is seen, and the self is 'realised,' so to speak, yet there may be little observerable change to lifestyle or appearance. There cannot be any criteria or formula for this. Yet the mind would seek just that – something it can do to attain something. There is no attainment whatsoever in present being, attainment is merely an idea of present deficiency in time.

What authority do you have to proclaim this as truth or wisdom?

Absolutely none whatsoever. To whom is this question addressed and by who? I will say once again this is not about hierarchy, there are no levels in being, it is void of any concept or notion of authority, be it of teaching of leading or following. This is all happening instantly, spontaneously – who does it? No-one!

Freedom is without structure and *being is freedom*. If there is a seeking of authority then that will be the appearance, but it suggests a dualistic right/wrong ideology rooted in opinion. Present awareness has no need of authority it is whole and complete in and of itself. It may be noticed that always these answers involve observing that time is the illusion, without which these questions and answers are moot and dissolve into one another. The paradox is, of course, that this is the dance of One - by many - in time.

No authority is necessary and none is possible. These are only concepts and symbols within the dance of life that give the appearance of drama – it's fun – really!

How can I tell which teaching holds truth from those which only purport to?

Who seeks a teaching? 'You' don't even look for a teacher at all, that is the appearance. Simply know that you are that which you seek right now, there is no need of a teacher or guru or any amount of knowledge or guidance for this to be so. This seems to be the most difficult thing for the character-identified-mind to accept. No teaching is better than another for any teaching is an ignorance of present perfection and unicity. If a teacher is sought however, then that will be what occurs as a manifestation of that perfection. Simply see the immediacy of being – that is it – this is all there is - simple!

So what is enlightenment?

Clarity - The timeless now - This!

Surely death is real and unavoidable.

Nothing in time has reality, it only appears in an instant to be followed by a seeming succession of 'other' instants, there is only now. Who would die? A character in time? The temporal character is a total fiction arising in pure being. Pure being is not temporal and not subject to change. Death of identification with the story is actually acute freedom. The apparent character does not have to appear to die for this to occur however.

There is only one thing that is unavoidable, and that is this very moment! Death of a body is the appearance, and so what?

Dialogues

But what if I loved that person and was distraught at their loss, surely that would mean something more than just this awfully cold sounding 'appearance?'

The temporal mind, the character, - who you think you are, is able to experience many many things, a whole variety and array of deep emotion and feeling. There is absolutely no denying the immense gravity of both pleasure and pain that can be felt within this temporal drama. But does it mean anything per se? Does it carry more credibility to suffer enormous loss or to be cold and nonchalant to all of life's happenings? Absolutely not. But it is the time-mind by it's very nature, which seeks to demand otherwise, to imbue life with this characteristic of hierarchy, of degree's and of levels and this is solely because of its polarised stance.

The actions of life, which includes emotion and feeling, are not in question, let them be what they will be. If great sadness is felt then there will be great sadness. If great joy, excitement or exhilaration are present, then likewise, that is what is present. Why seek to give meaning to the appearance? But this is just what the mind in time will do, seek meaning, because that is it's nature and how the game of relativity is played. It is a judgmental mind, an assessor, an evaluator and a seeker-outside-of-now. And as absurd as that may be, it is perfectly okay.

Let it be. Just let life be as it will. And perhaps the perfection may be glimpsed within the tumult and the drama?

But suffering feels very real, pain feels very real, sometimes all this intellectualising doesn't seem to help at all, or give me anything of substance I can use to avoid suffering.

Of course appearances take many forms as I have said over and over. But what makes suffering suffering, is *interpreting* experience as something to be avoided. This all begins with identification with this personal entity-in-time that can seem to choose. It can't! It doesn't! It is on a roller coaster ride without choice, to be enjoyed not fought against! But if fighting is present – so be it.

Suffering is ignorance, ignorance of being. Suffering is the outcome of deception. Suffering is the appearance of volitional form, yet from has no volition, no choice.

Intellectualising likewise is part of the dance it can never give 'you' anything because it *is as much you as everything else.* You are not finite concept. If you seek only pleasure, you attract pain in equal measure, but only through conceptual interpretation – through seeing things that way, identifying things from you own particular perspective – these are the illusions – the interpretations. It is the infinite dance.

DIALOGUES

If I become more loving to others and more charitable as some doctrines suggest, will I have greater clarity and be able to approach present awareness easier?

No! Again 'You' can *do* nothing and *need do* nothing! This fictitious 'you' is only an idea. What you are is clarity, is being, is awareness, is One. This is not an achievable 'state,' but the ground of being behind all, and giving rise to all. It can only be seen or otherwise. Yet both seeing and not seeing are, strangely, it too! Any attempt at behavioural change gives a seeming temporal reality to the individual that it does not posses. There is no individual chooser, no doer of the action. Life happens spontaneously. Only observation would possibly reveal this. The action is completely irrelevant and utterly meaningless. Intention implies an intender, the intender is a concept of mind. Notice that the perfection of life is happening right now! It may be true that the agitation of a mind at peace creates less resistance and conflict, but this again is the appearance and beyond any sense of volitional choosing.

If you find you are annoyed at something observe the annoyance without trying to label it as good or bad, see that the nature of the anger or annoyance has its own kind of feel or flavour. Perhaps you may become more interested in the nature of that feeling than in the labelling or judging of it – this detached observation may give rise to a certain clarity. Whether this occurs or not all we can say is.... we shall see?

Why even try to express what is, as you say, happening quite spontaneously anyway, what is the point?

The expressing of this dialogue between us *is happening spontaneously,* all of it is, you see?. *This is the dance!* Everything IS spontaneous. The 'why' question is once more a question in time, and hence a seeking to establish reason and a reasoner, a path and destination which do not exist within this immediate dance. And of course, there is absolutely no point, nowhere to get to or to get from – you are here now – always. There is no contradiction in presence.

Some scriptures talk of dropping the idea of being good, is this the final hurdle for the seeker?

Once more, *there are no levels. There is no hierarchy.* The path to attainment is a product only of time-mindedness. See that all striving and attaining is merely the avoidance of *what is.* Why assume you must attain or reach. This sense of life, of beingness, is complete and immediate. All actions or negations are simply more concepts or ways in which 'I' can *seem* to attain that which *seems* to be missing. What is there to attain - what is missing, Nothing! This is it!

Of course there are many 'spiritual paths,' each equally as misleading as the next for they are products of time or sequential doctrines describing routes an elevated state not present right now. It may even be proved that this or that person became 'self-realised' as a result of this or that particular set of rules. But this too is storytelling. But where is this story seen if not *right here and right now?* There is simply no getting away from immediate being.

Will an individual follow a certain path, who can say? There is no chooser after all, so why not just simply enjoy what happens, enjoy the decisions that seem to arise, lets just see. Religions are manufactured stories to give the drama further flavour that all good narratives possess. But after all this is all story anyway –so why not enjoy?

How do we know that all these words and concepts are not meaningless themselves?

Oh now wait a second, lets be clear about this, they are <u>*definitely meaningless*</u>! However, they may point towards something beyond conceptualisation, but of themselves they are nothing. It is the proverbial finger pointing at the moon, it is not the finger we need examine. Ultimately we simply dance.

Thank you.

You may contact the author by email at:
deon@blueyonder.co.uk